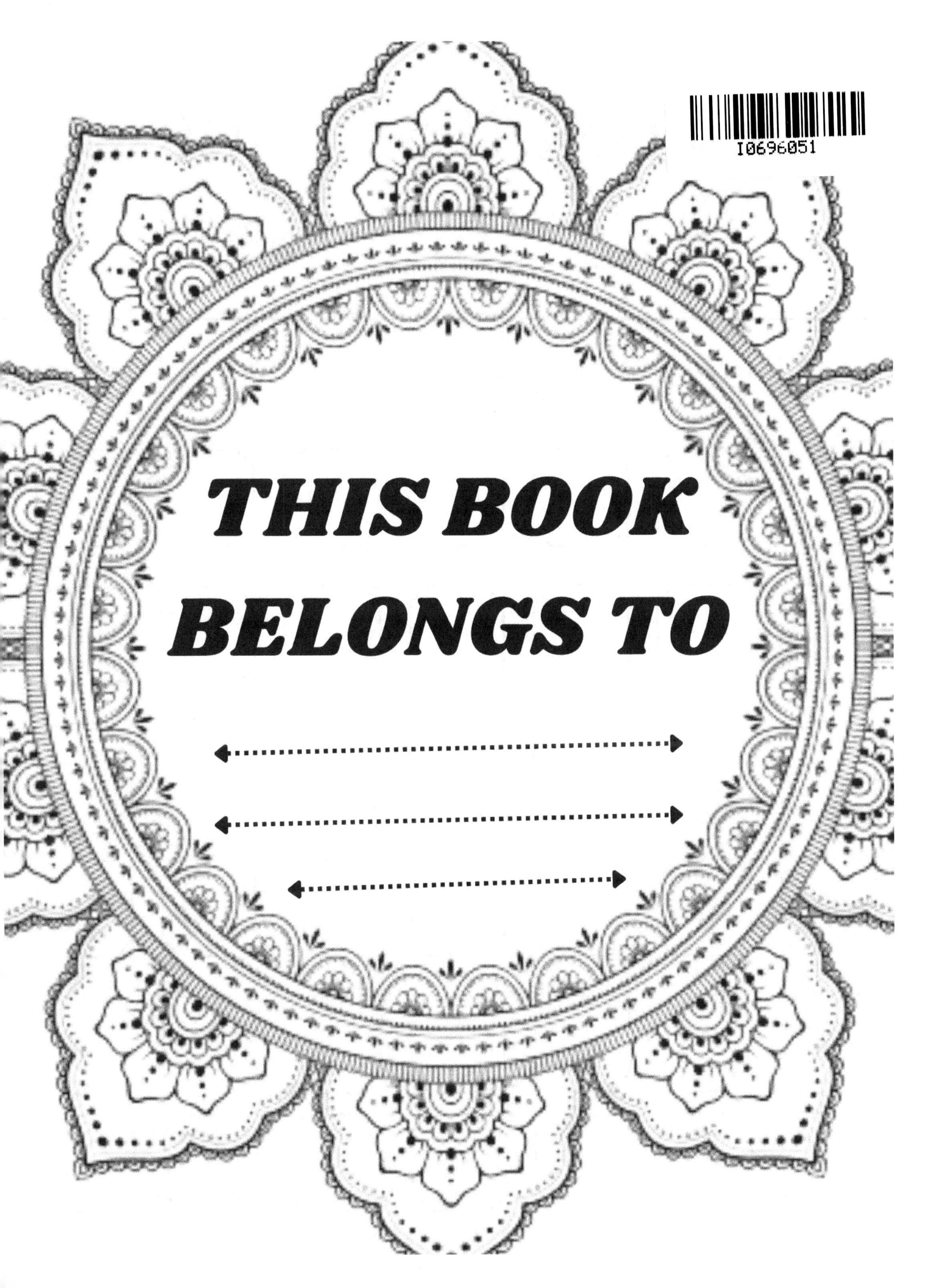
I0696051
THIS BOOK
BELONGS TO

COLOR TEST PAGE

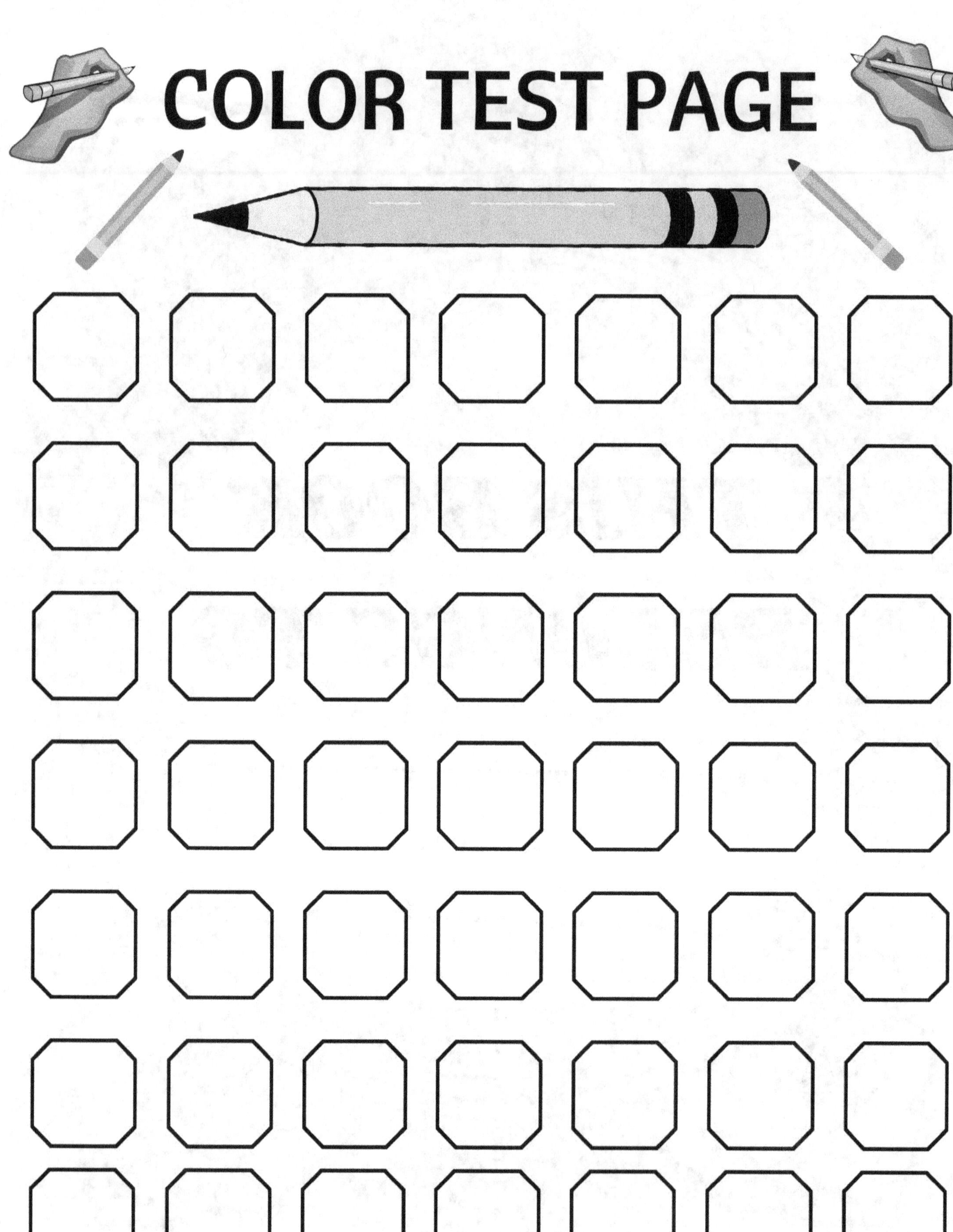

Color Test Page

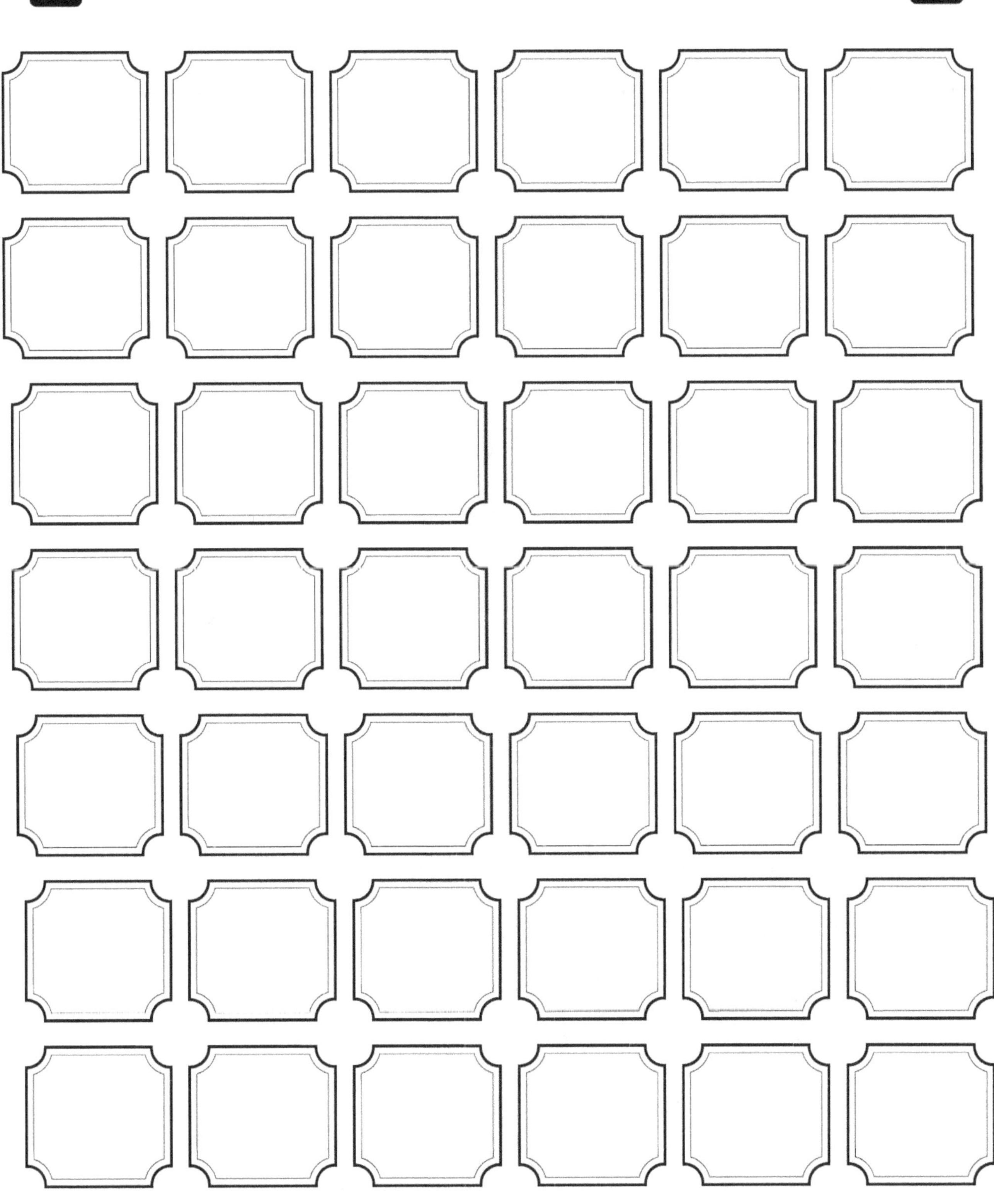

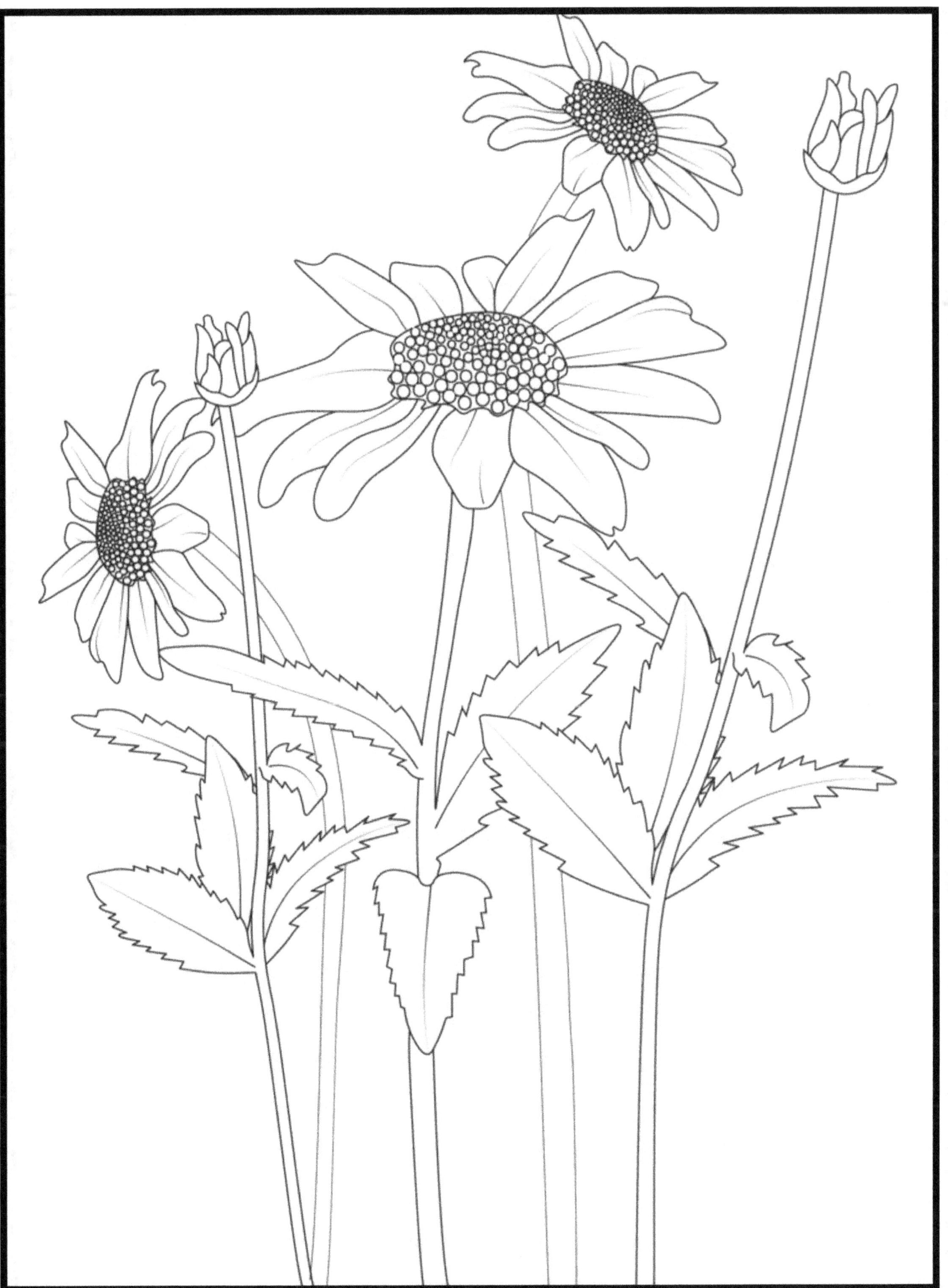

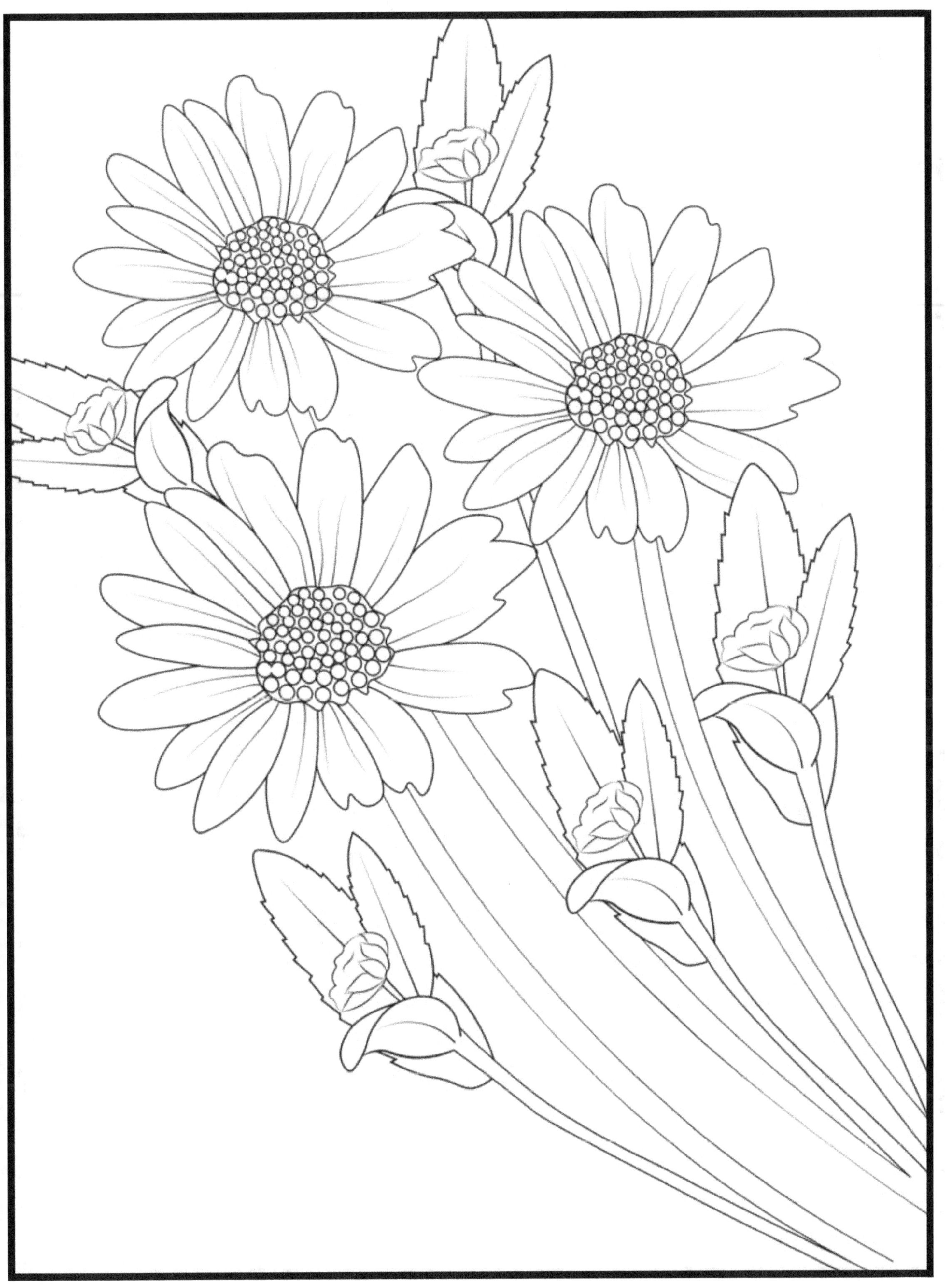

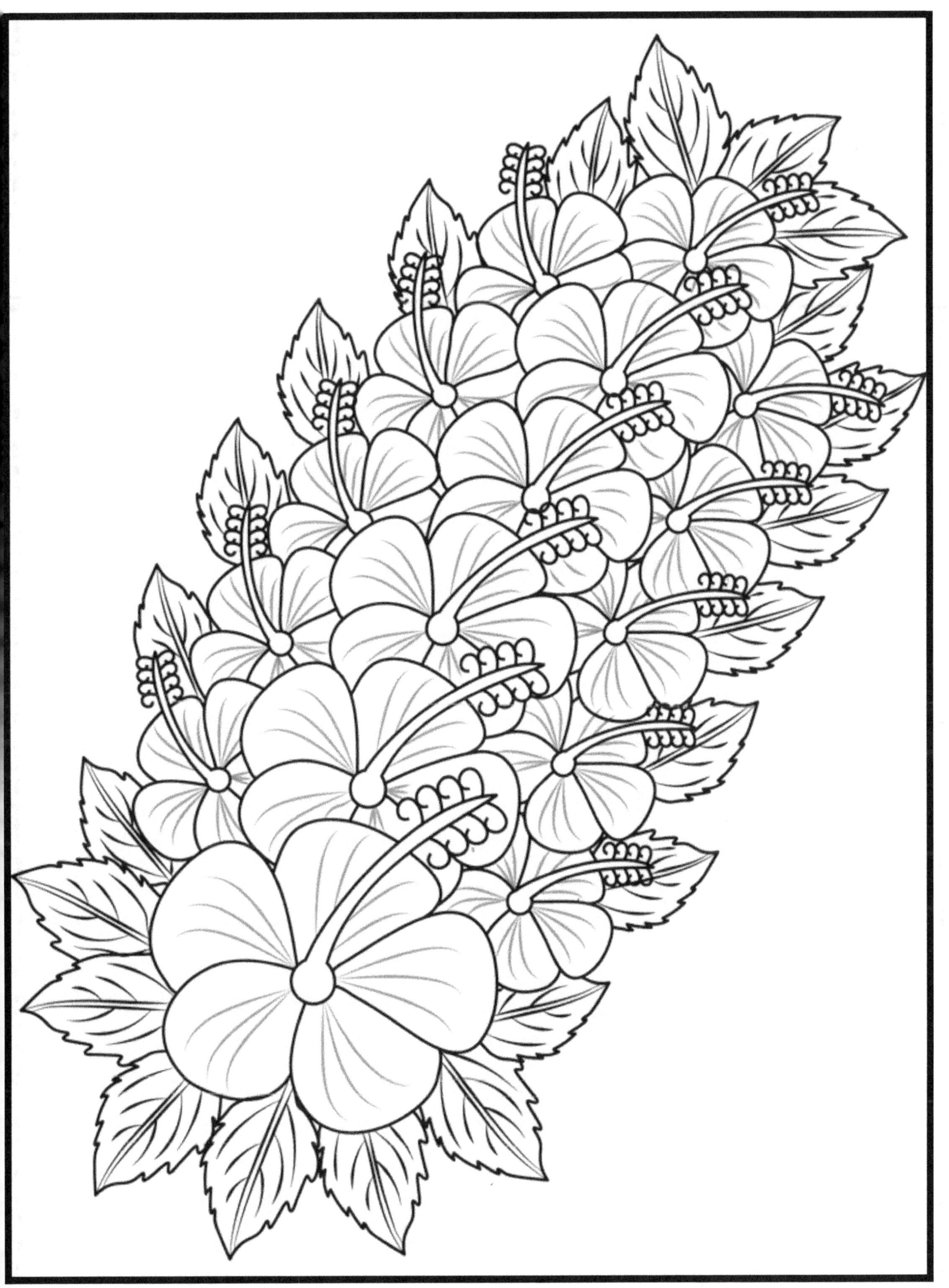

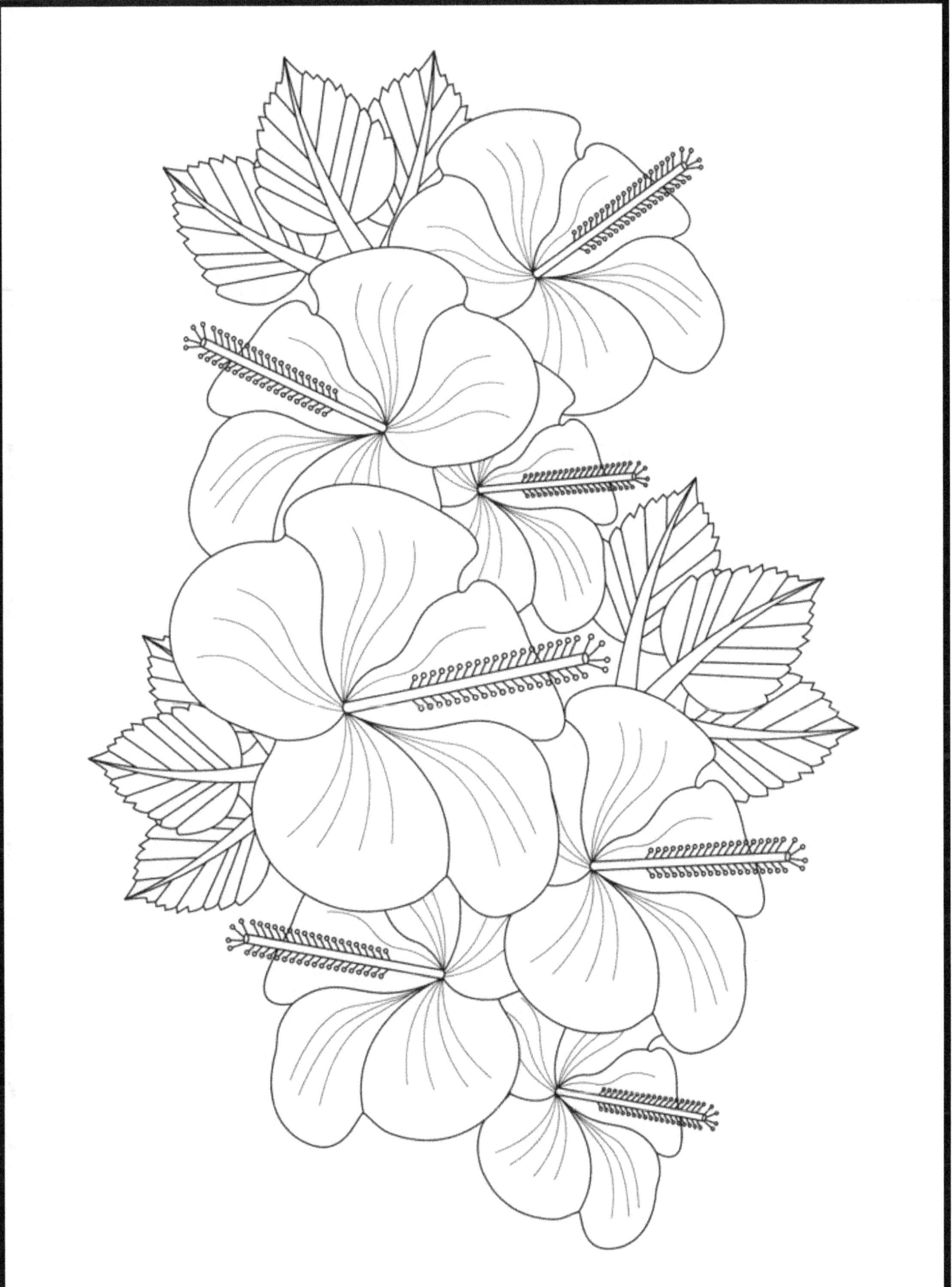

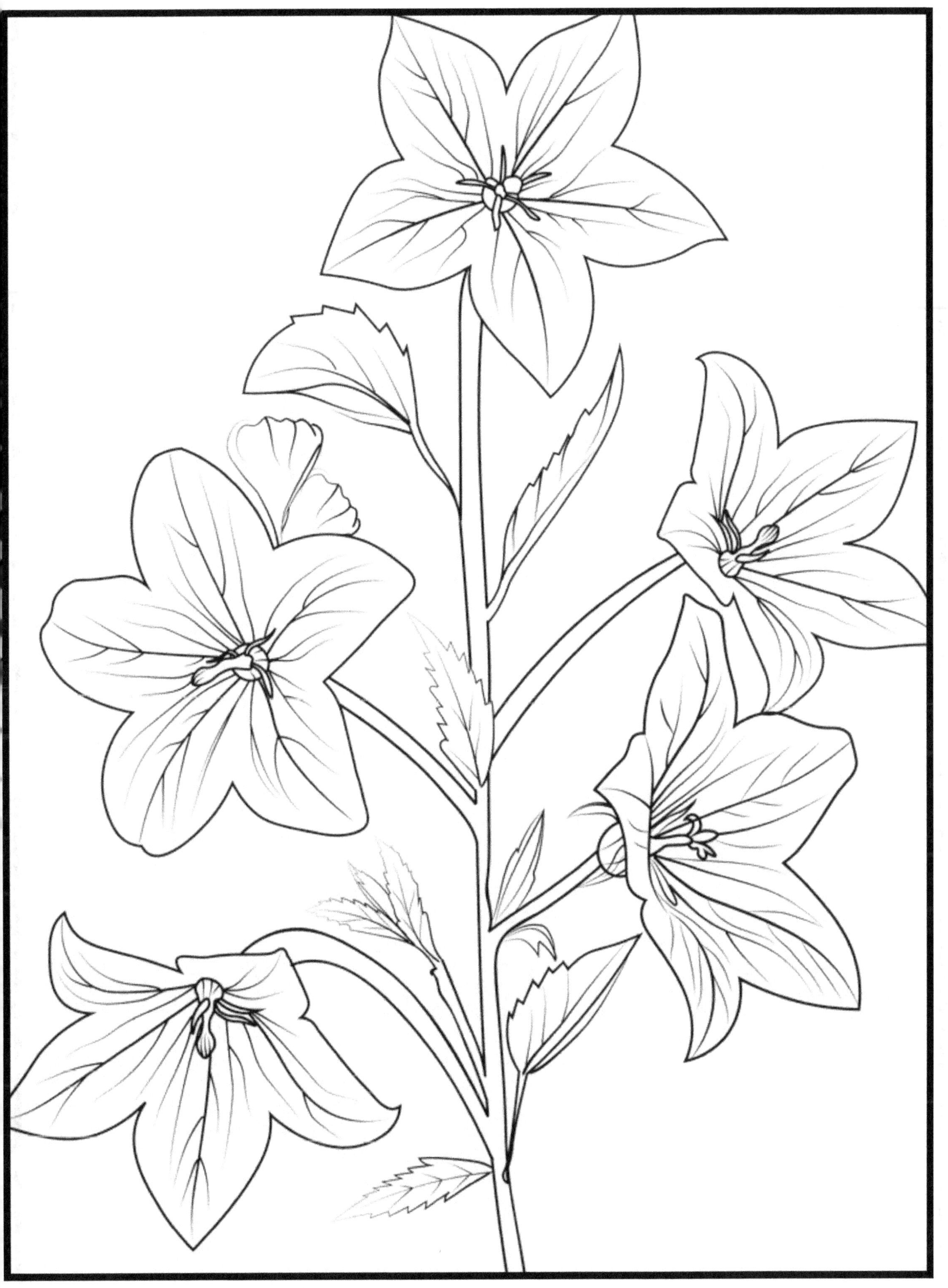

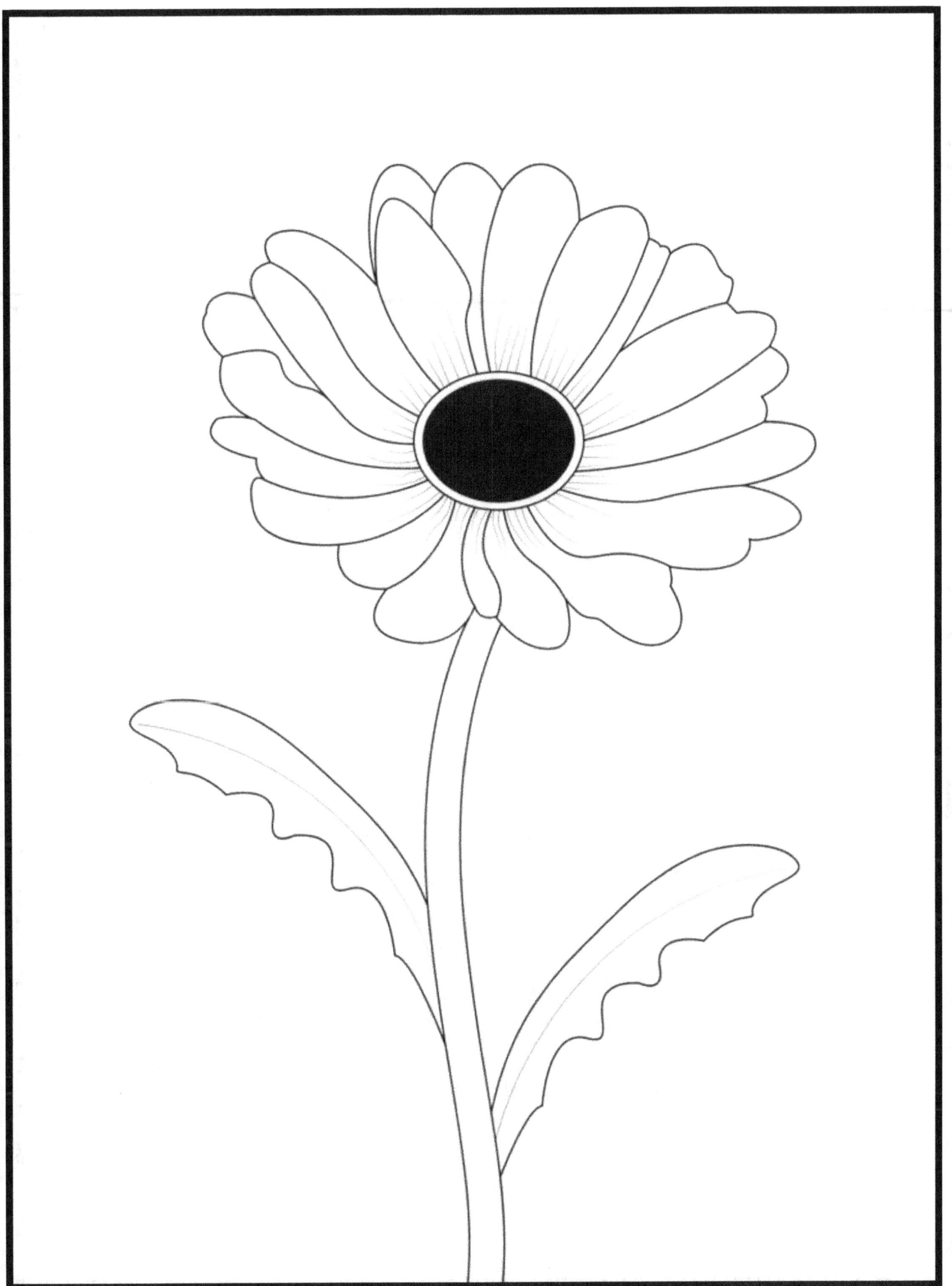

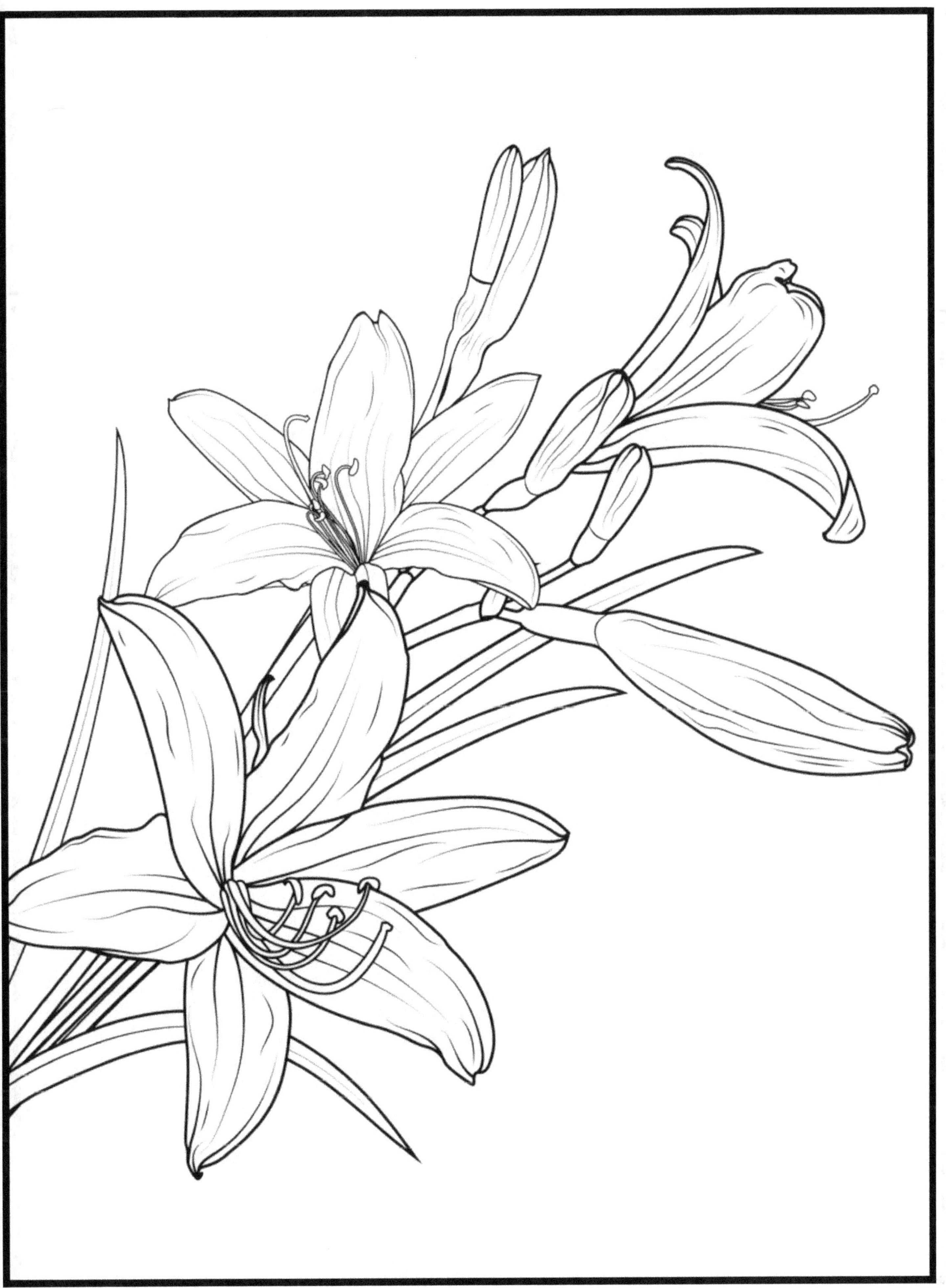

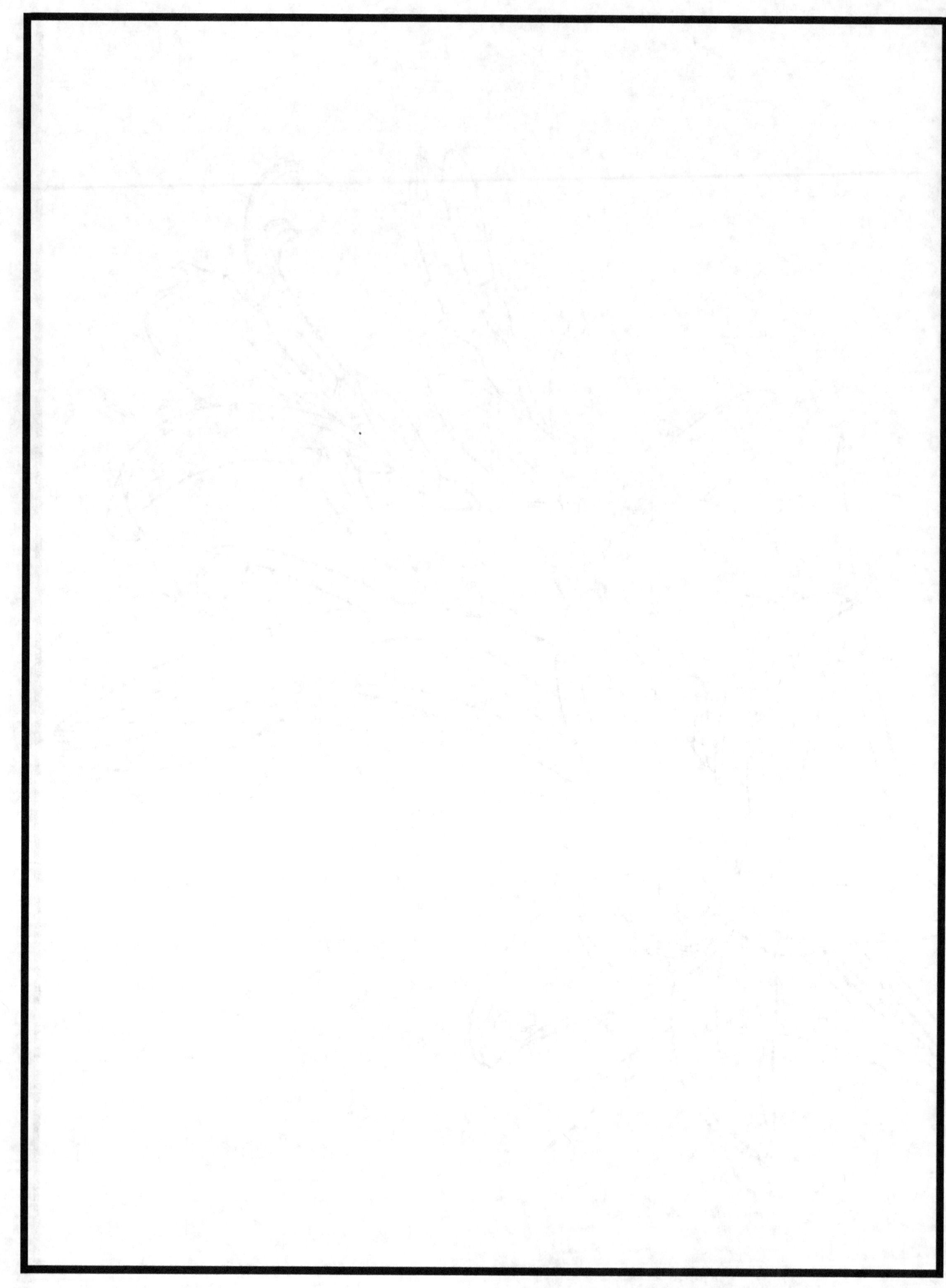

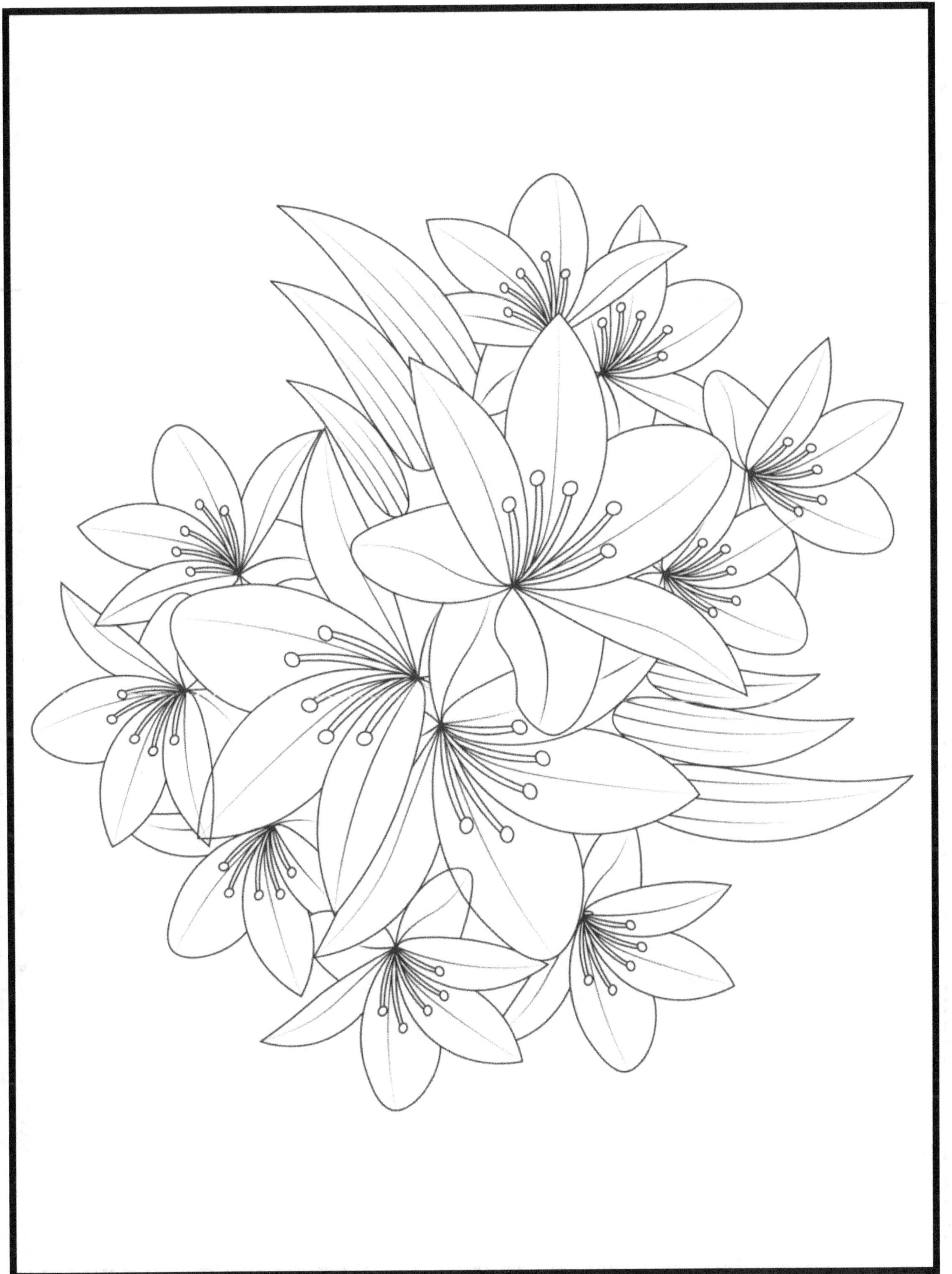

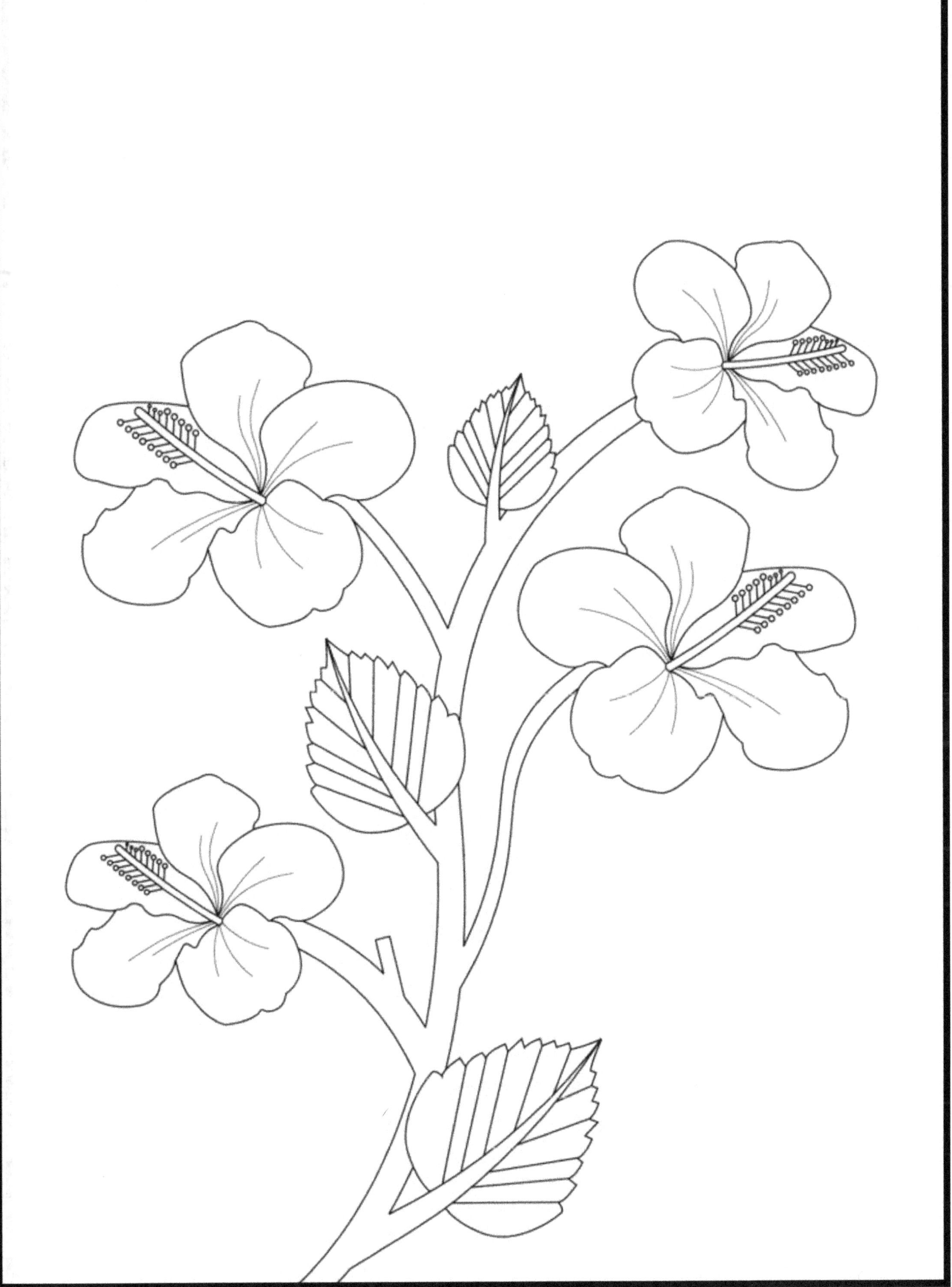

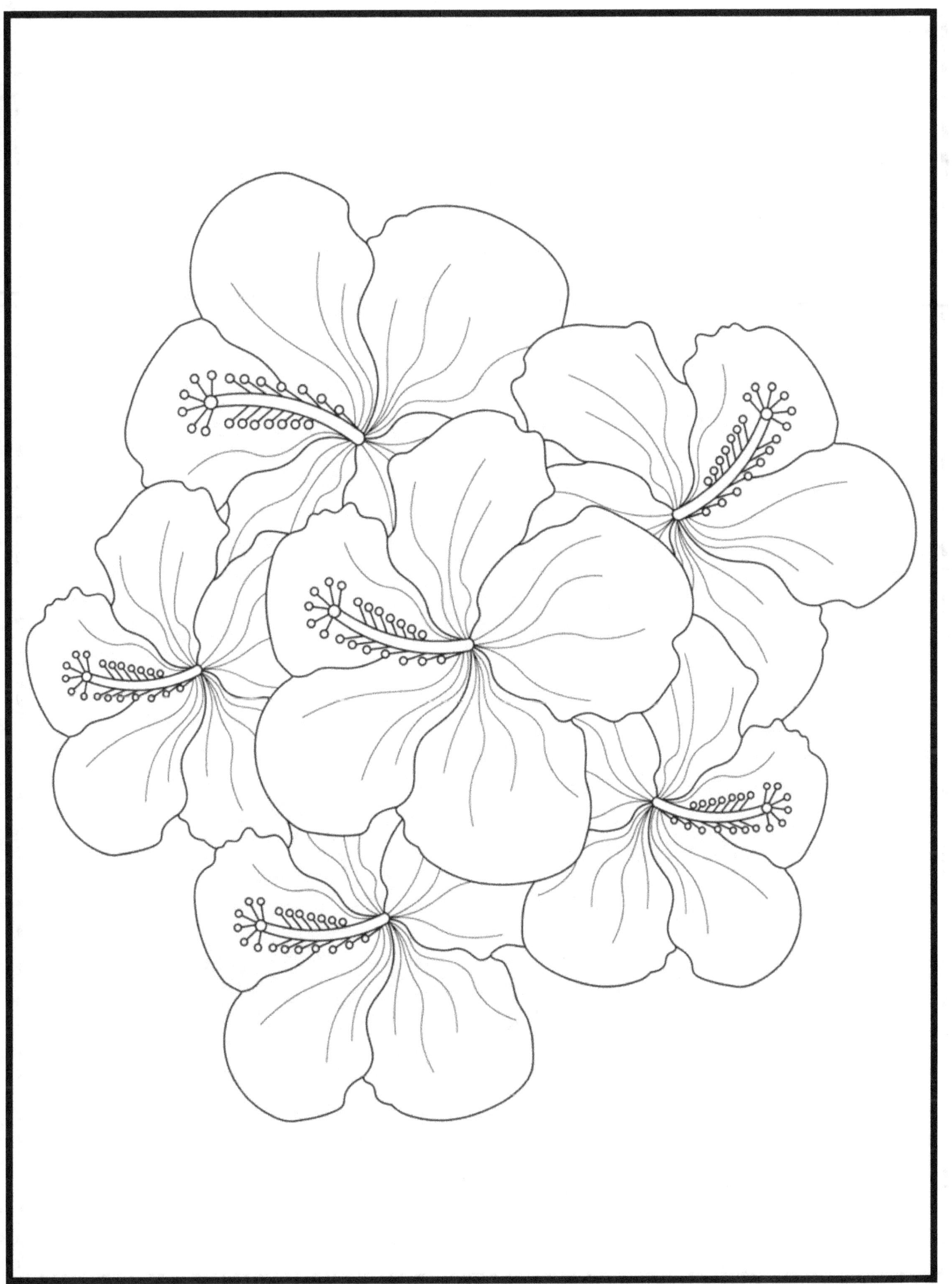

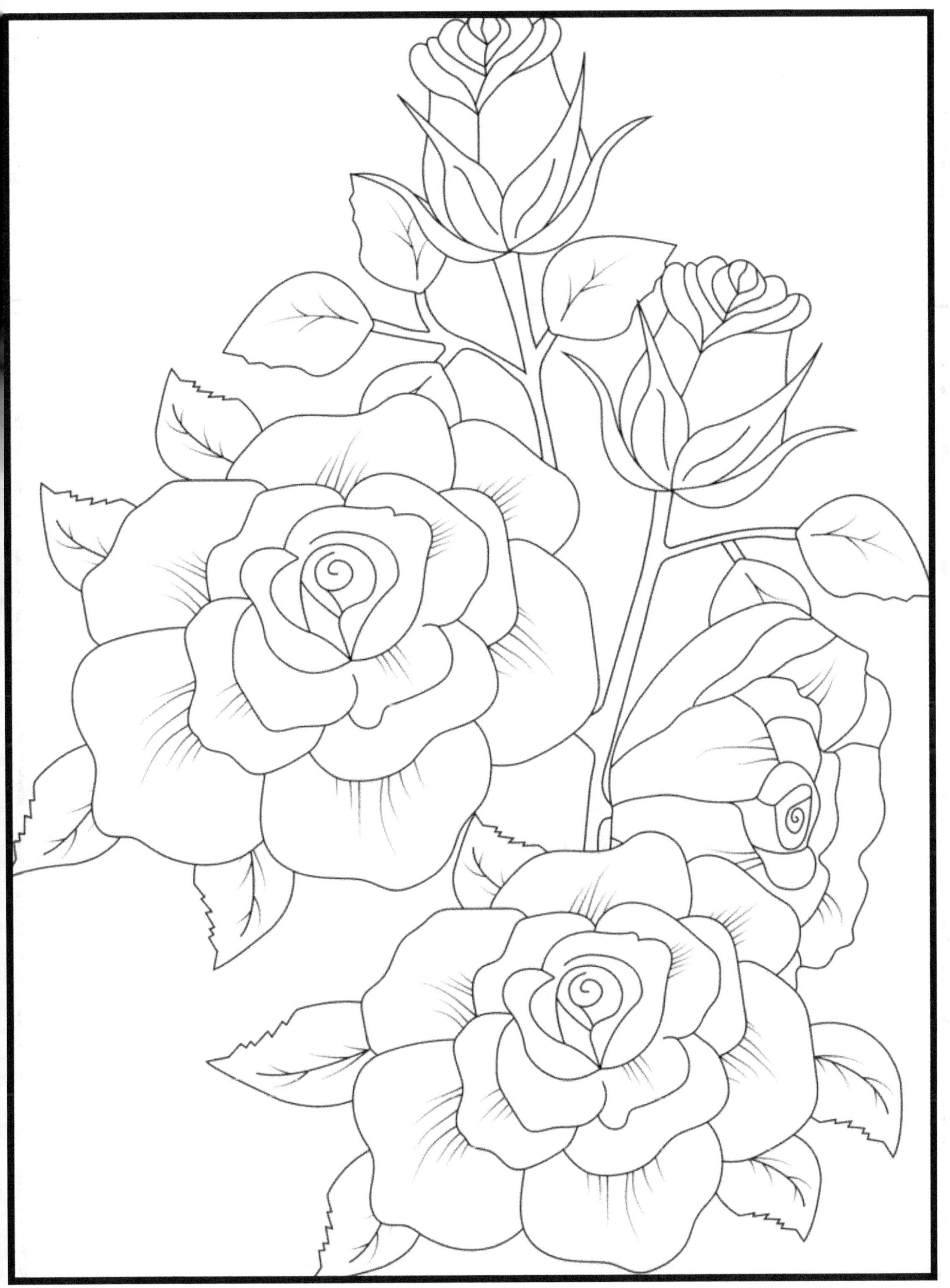

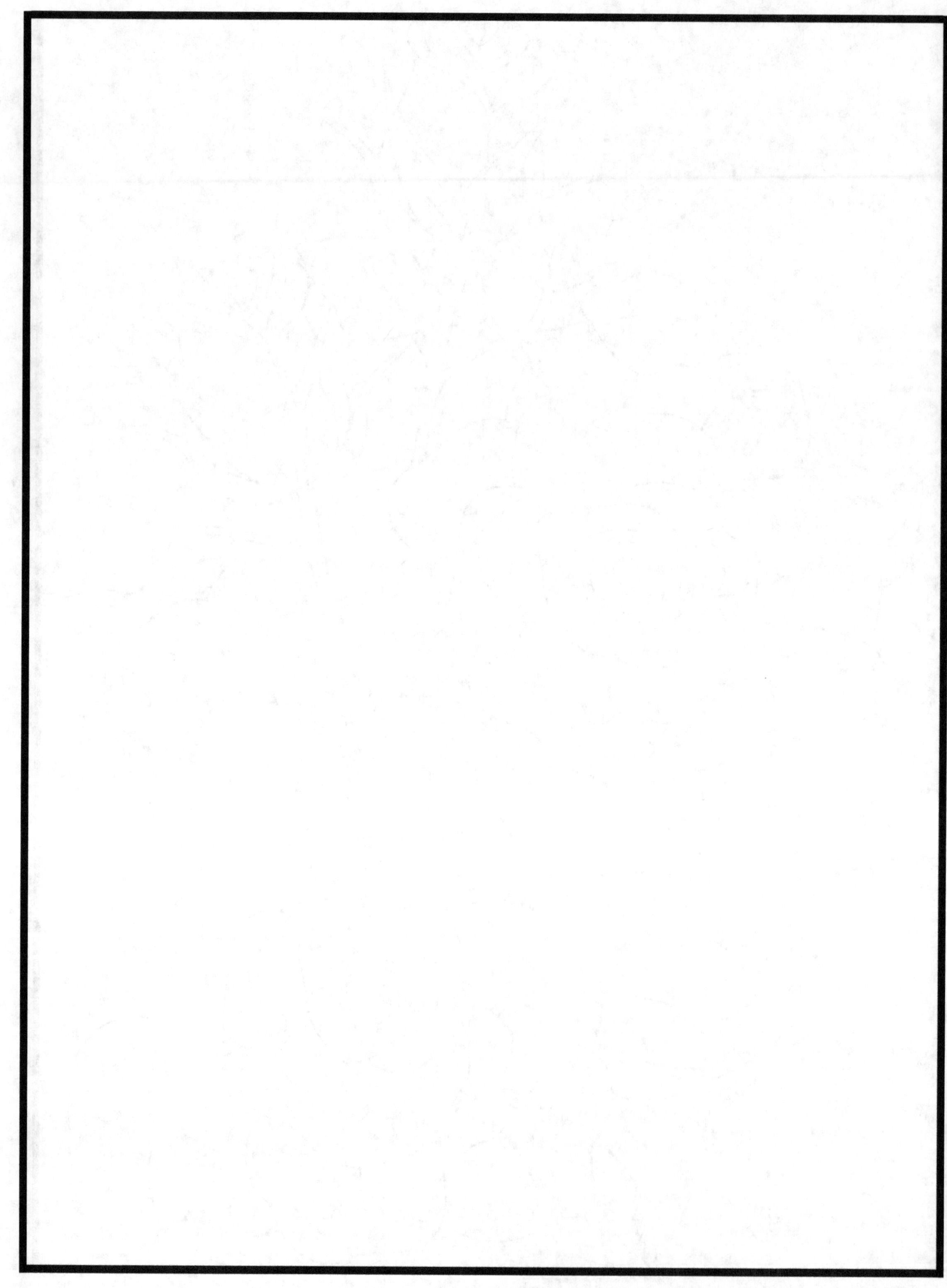

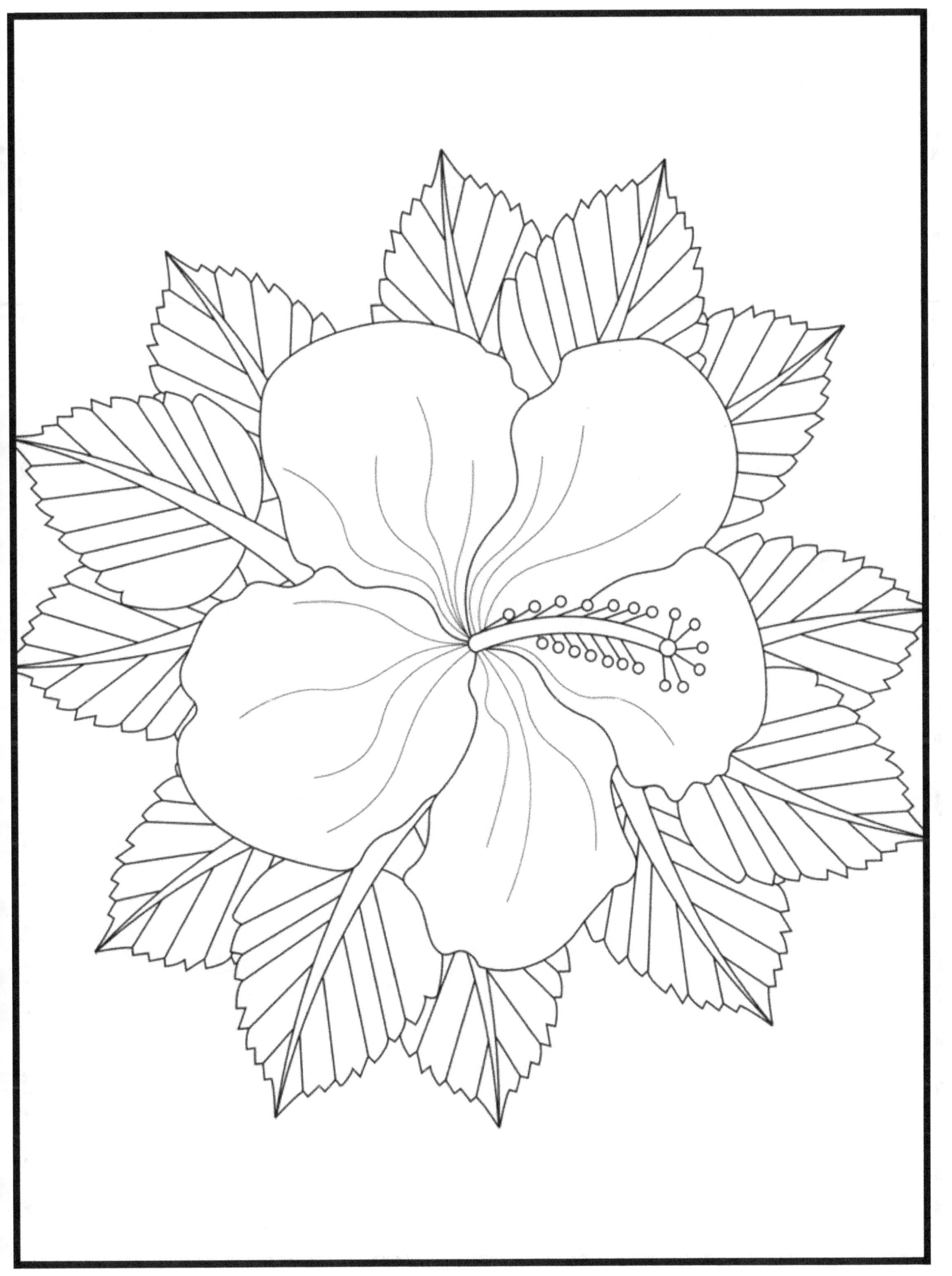

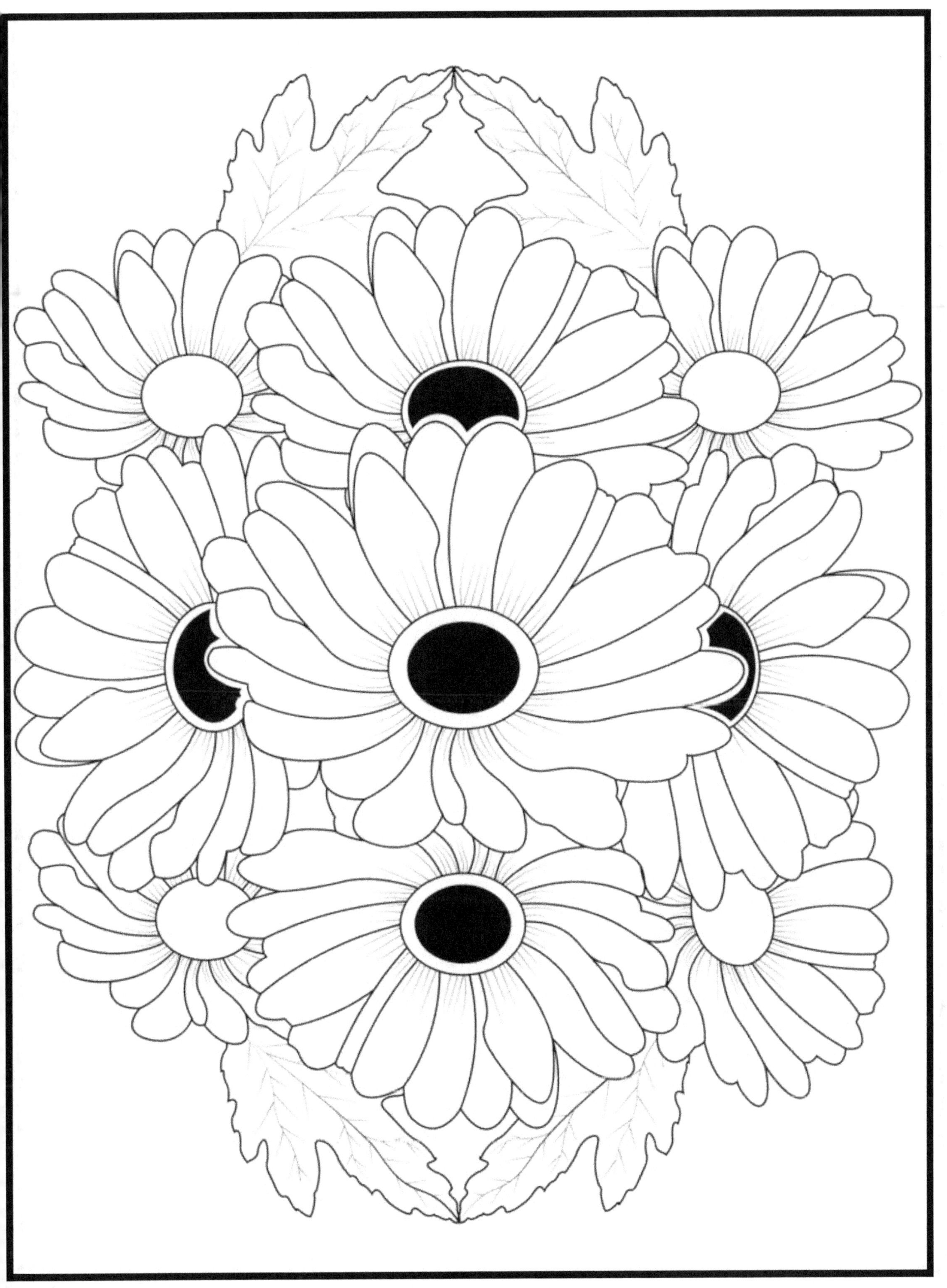

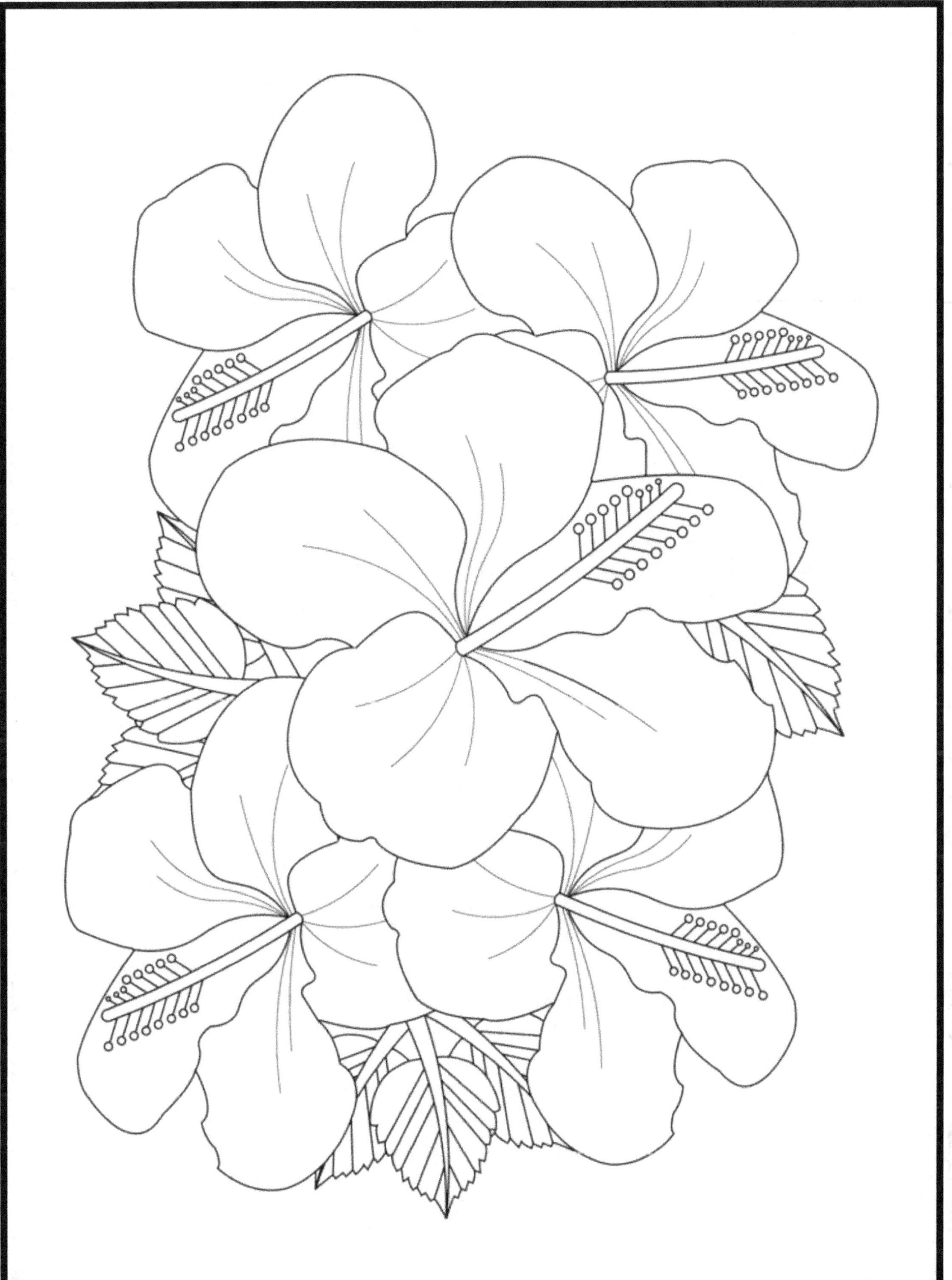

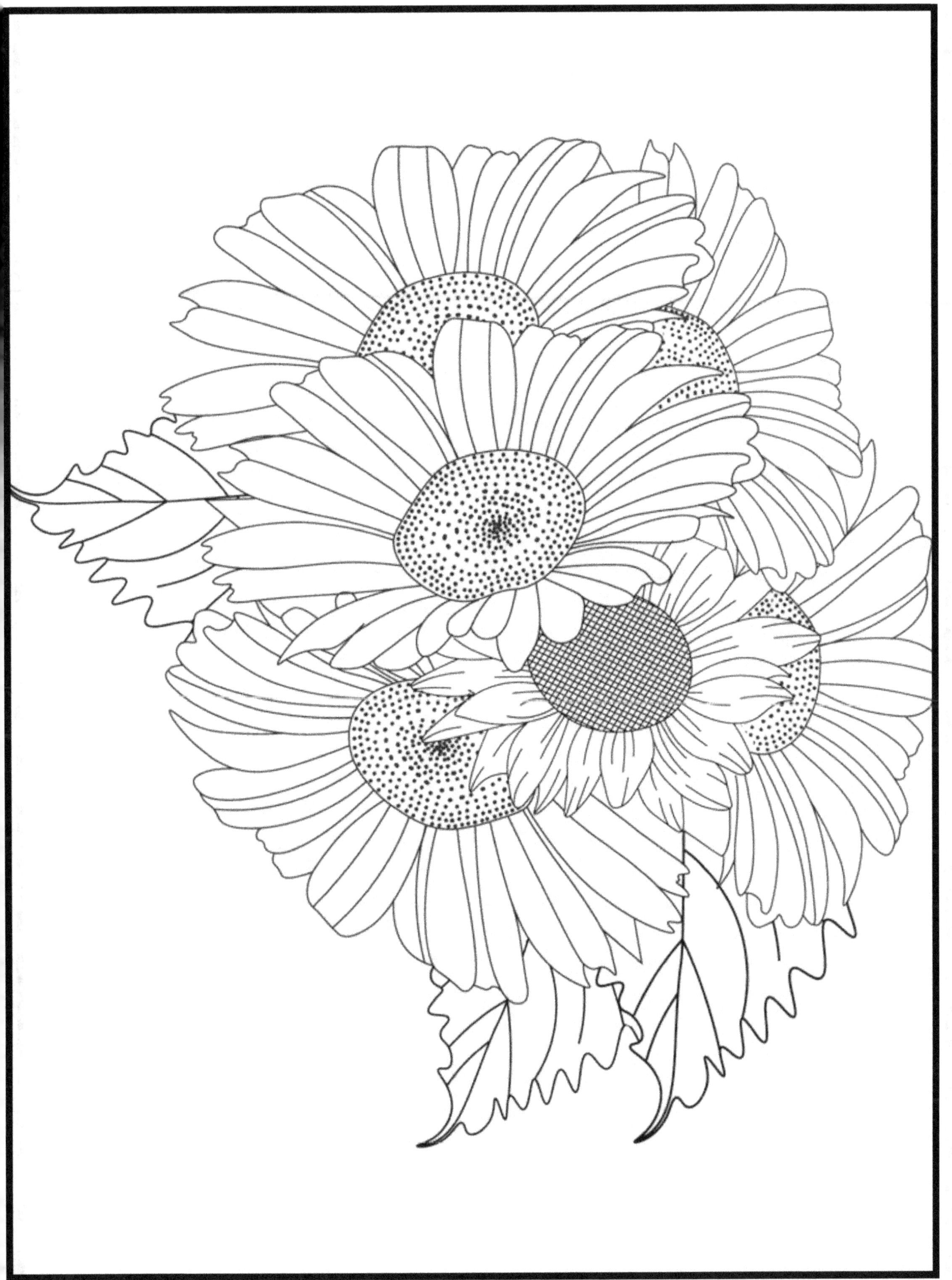

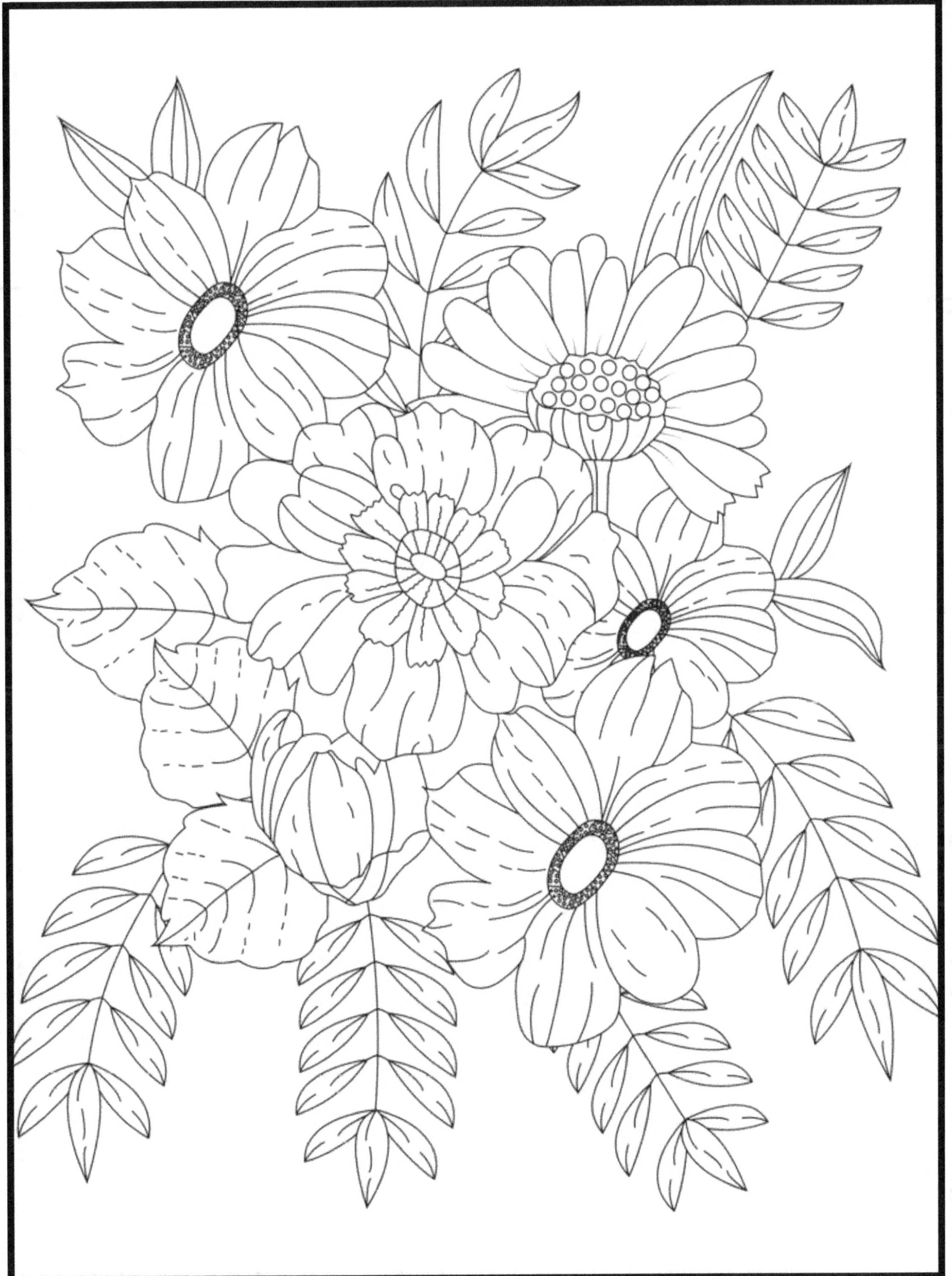

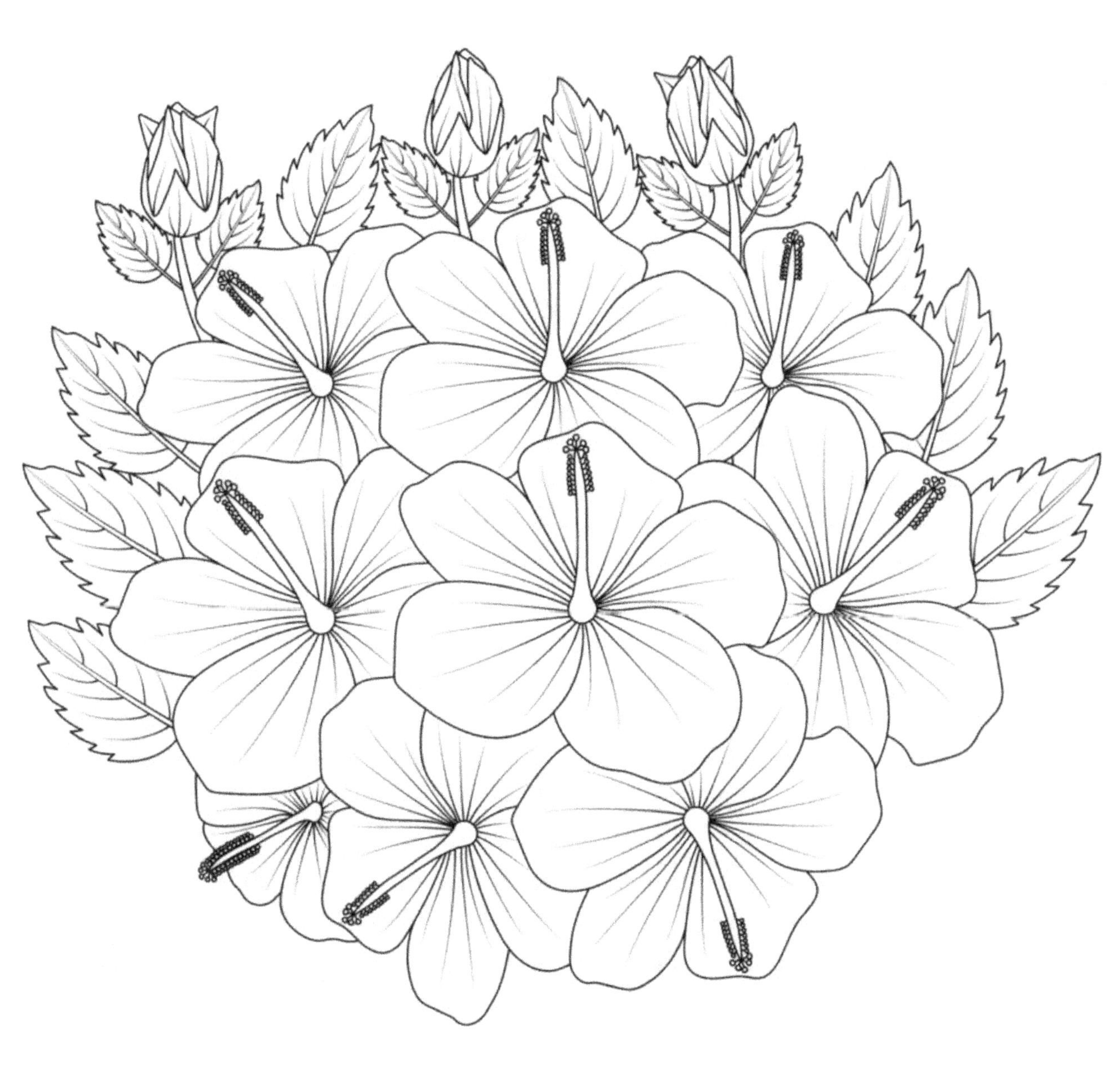

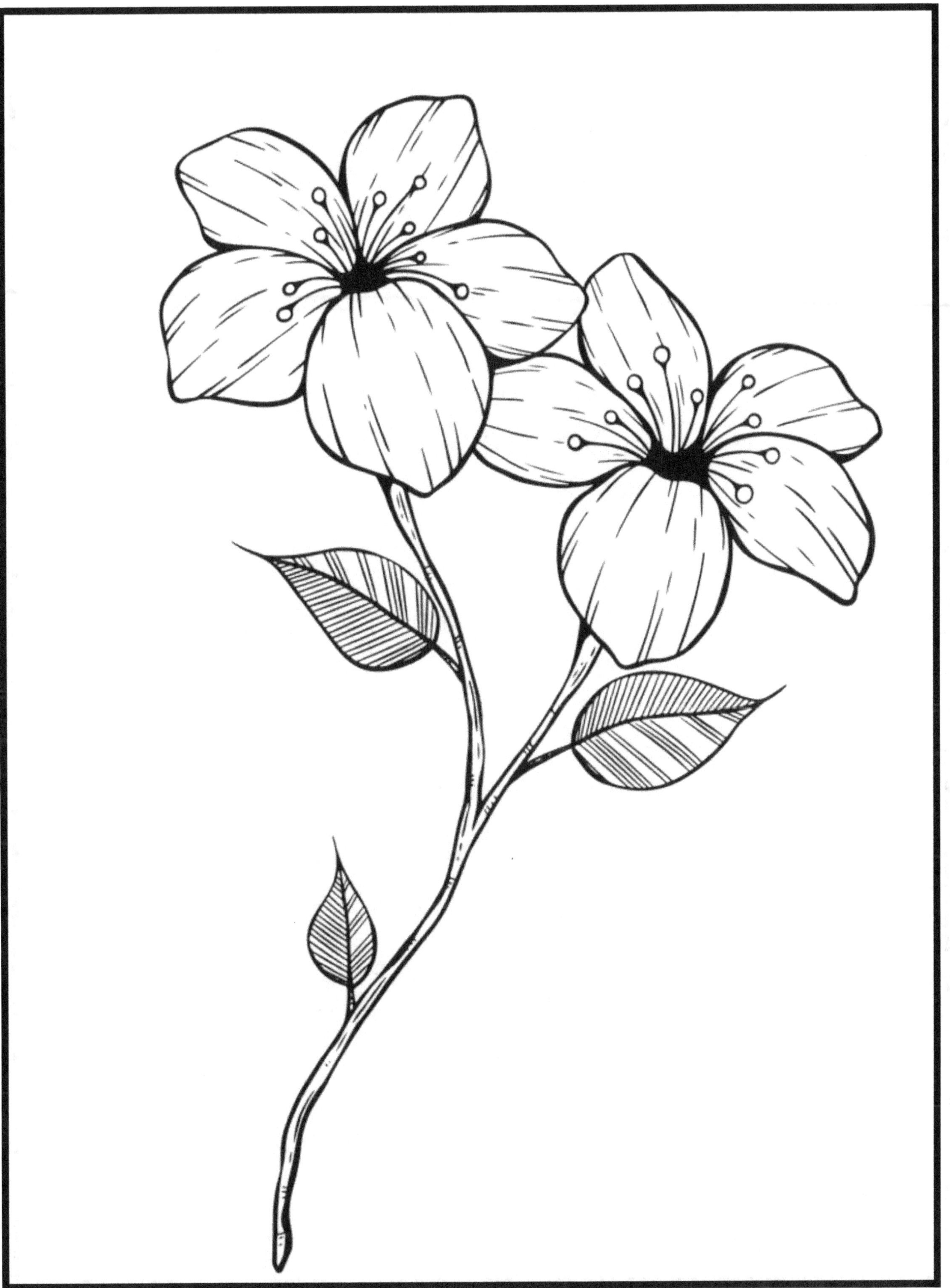

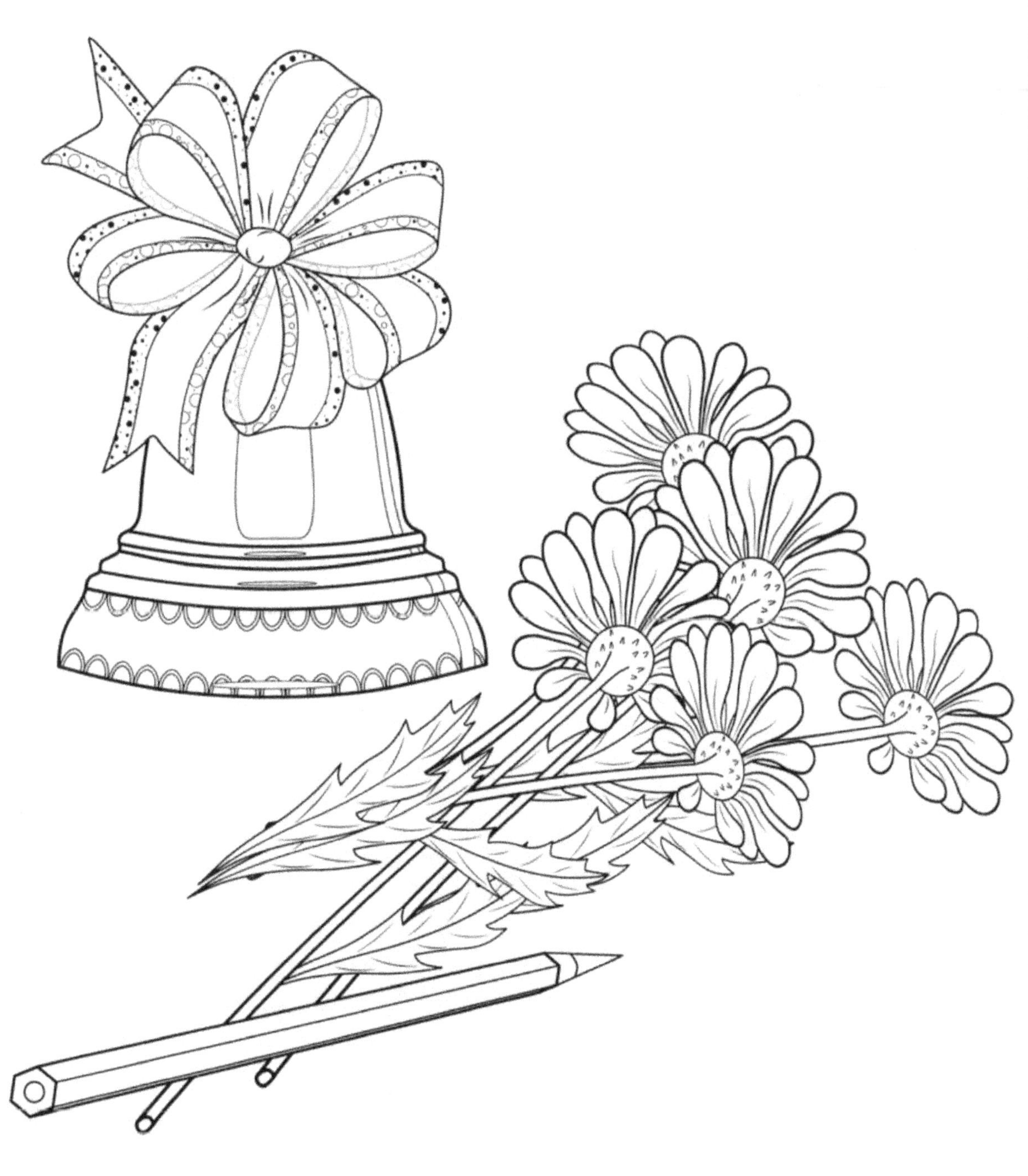

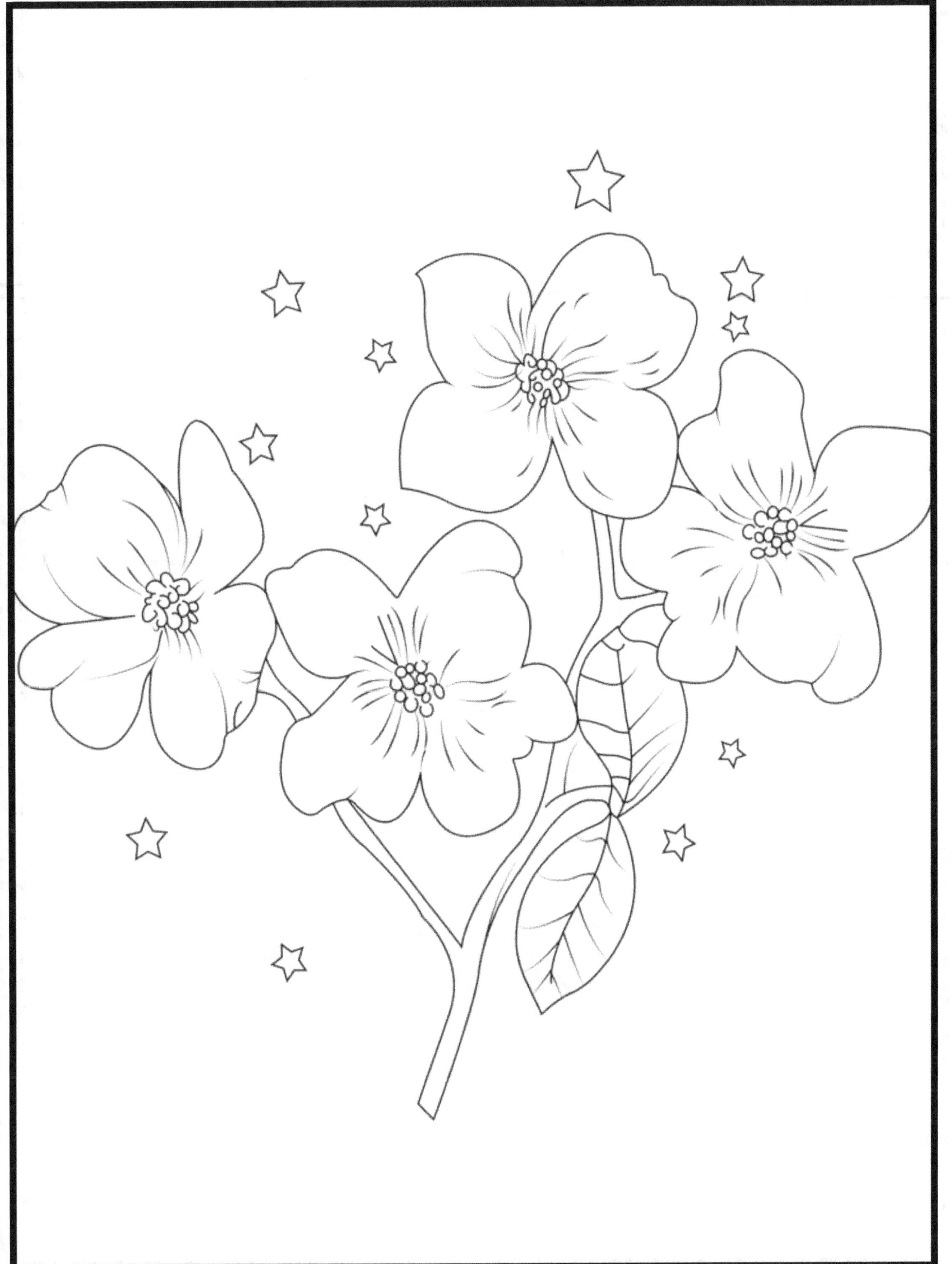

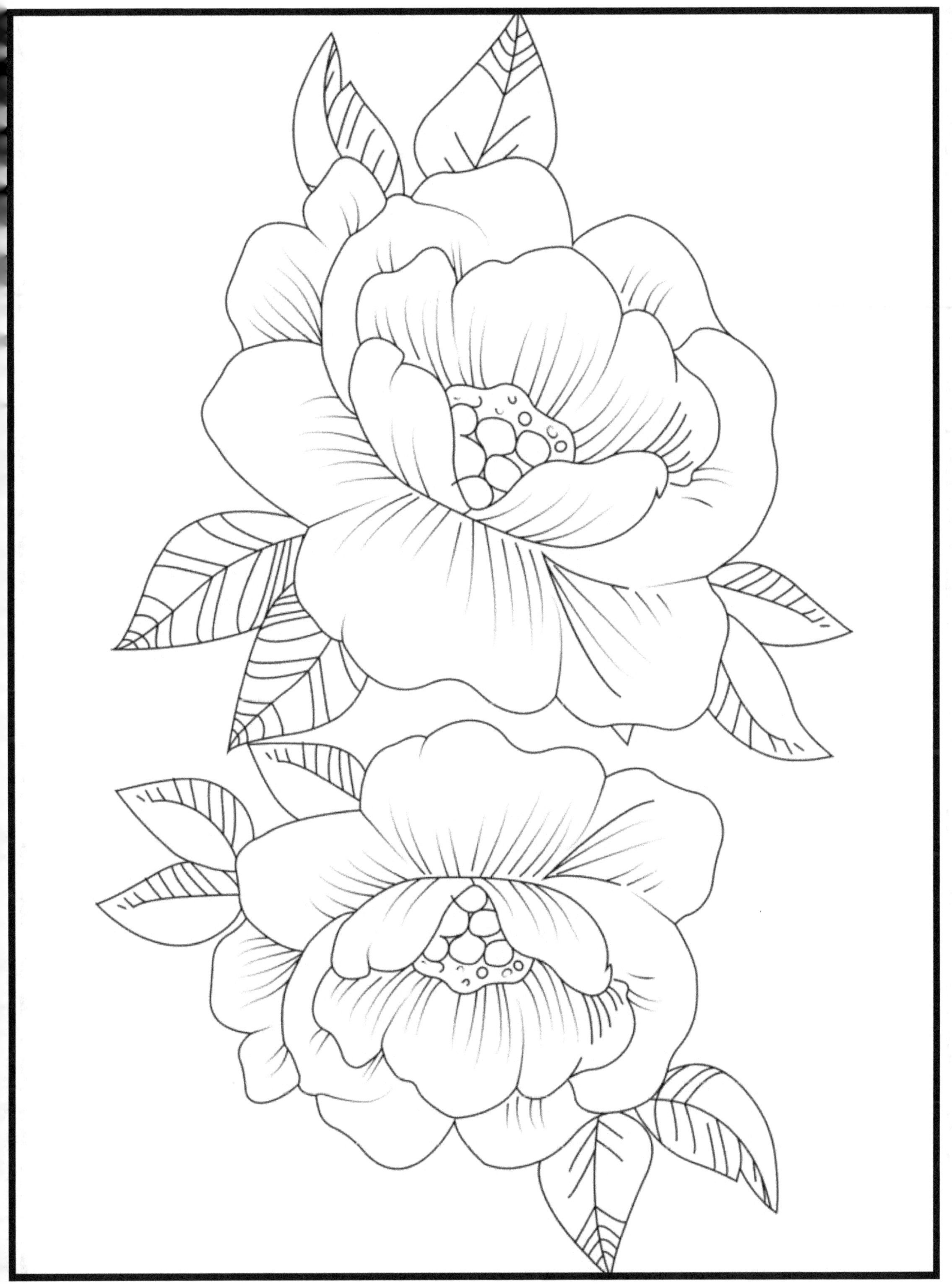

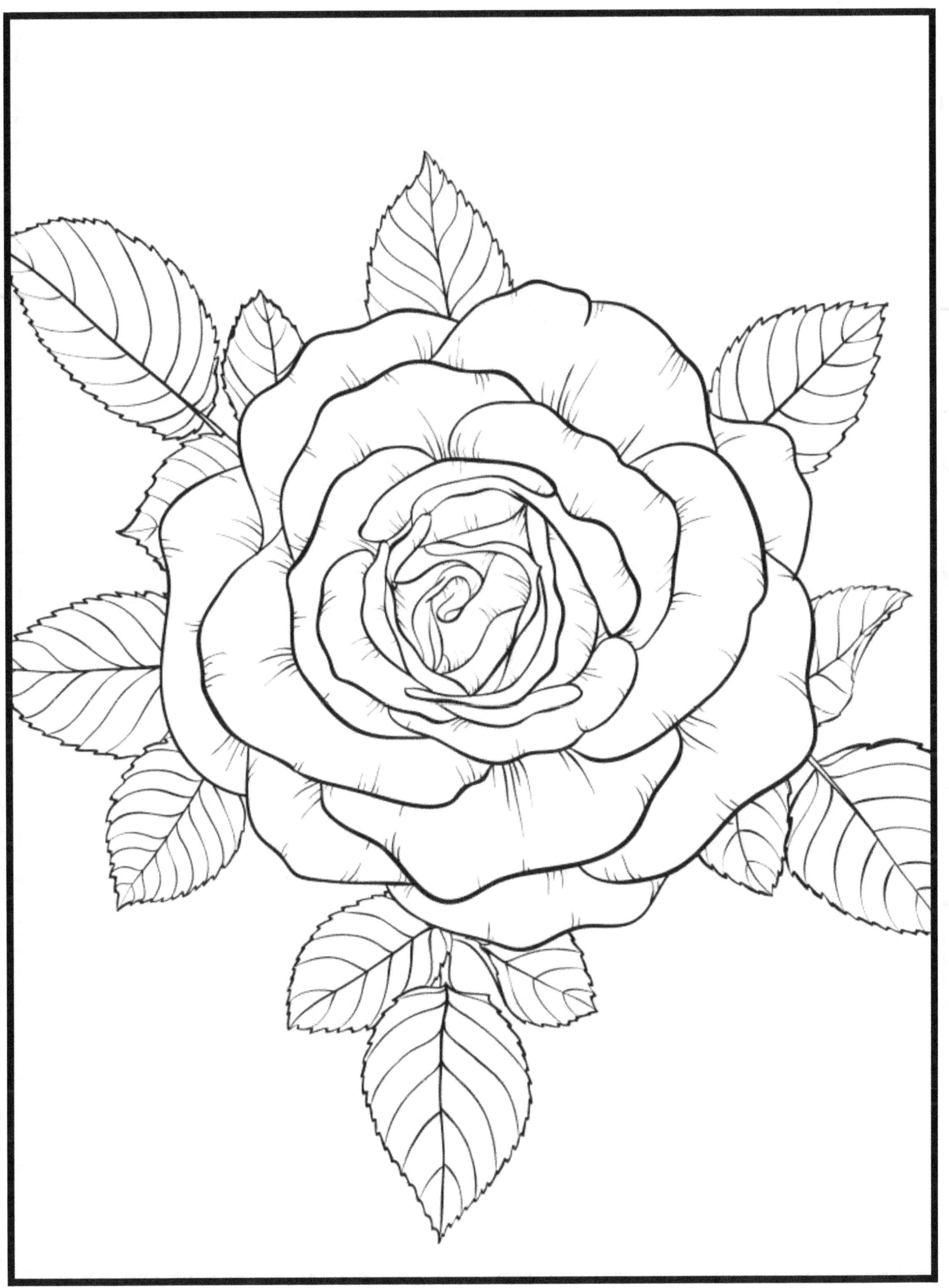

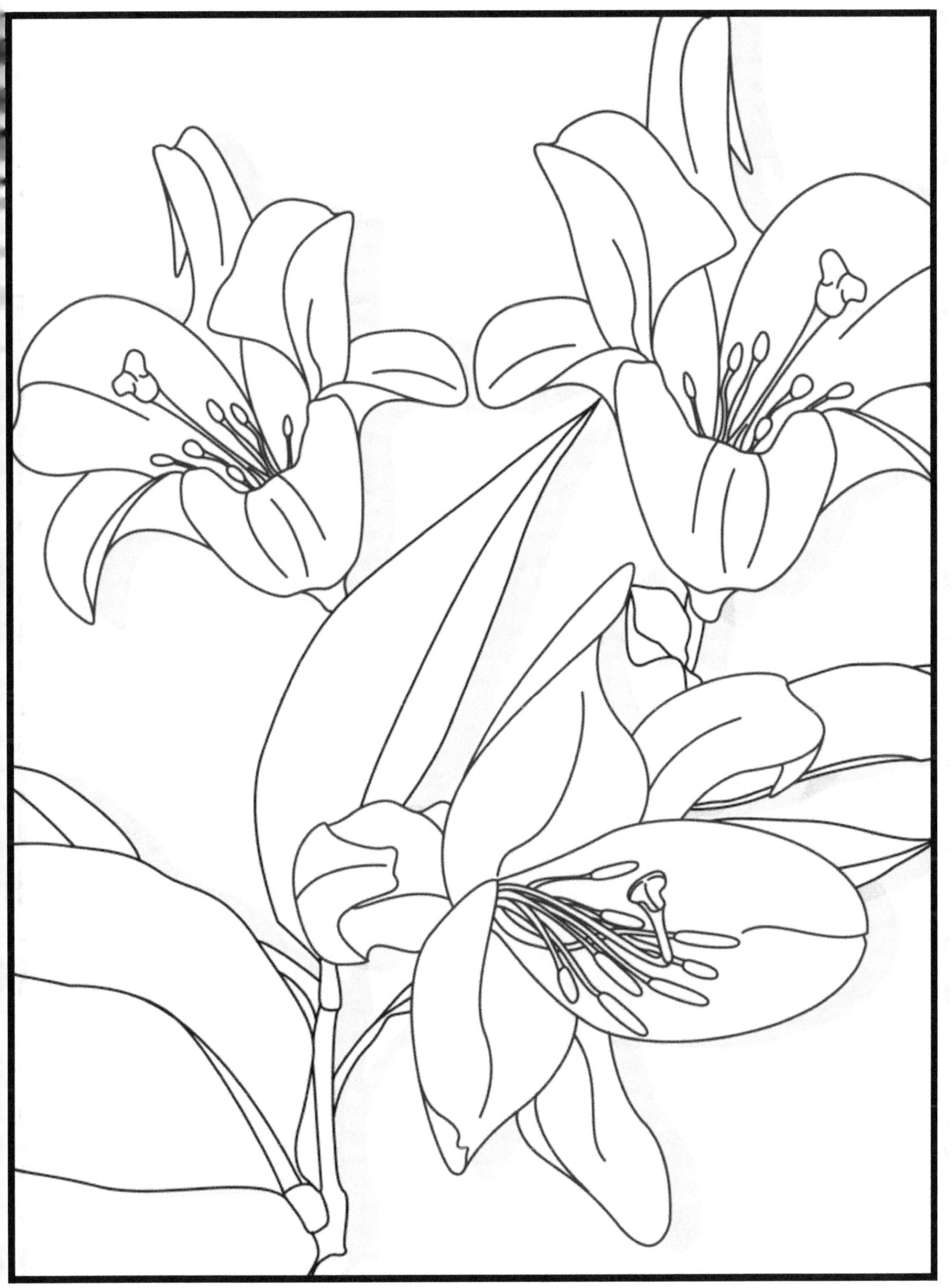

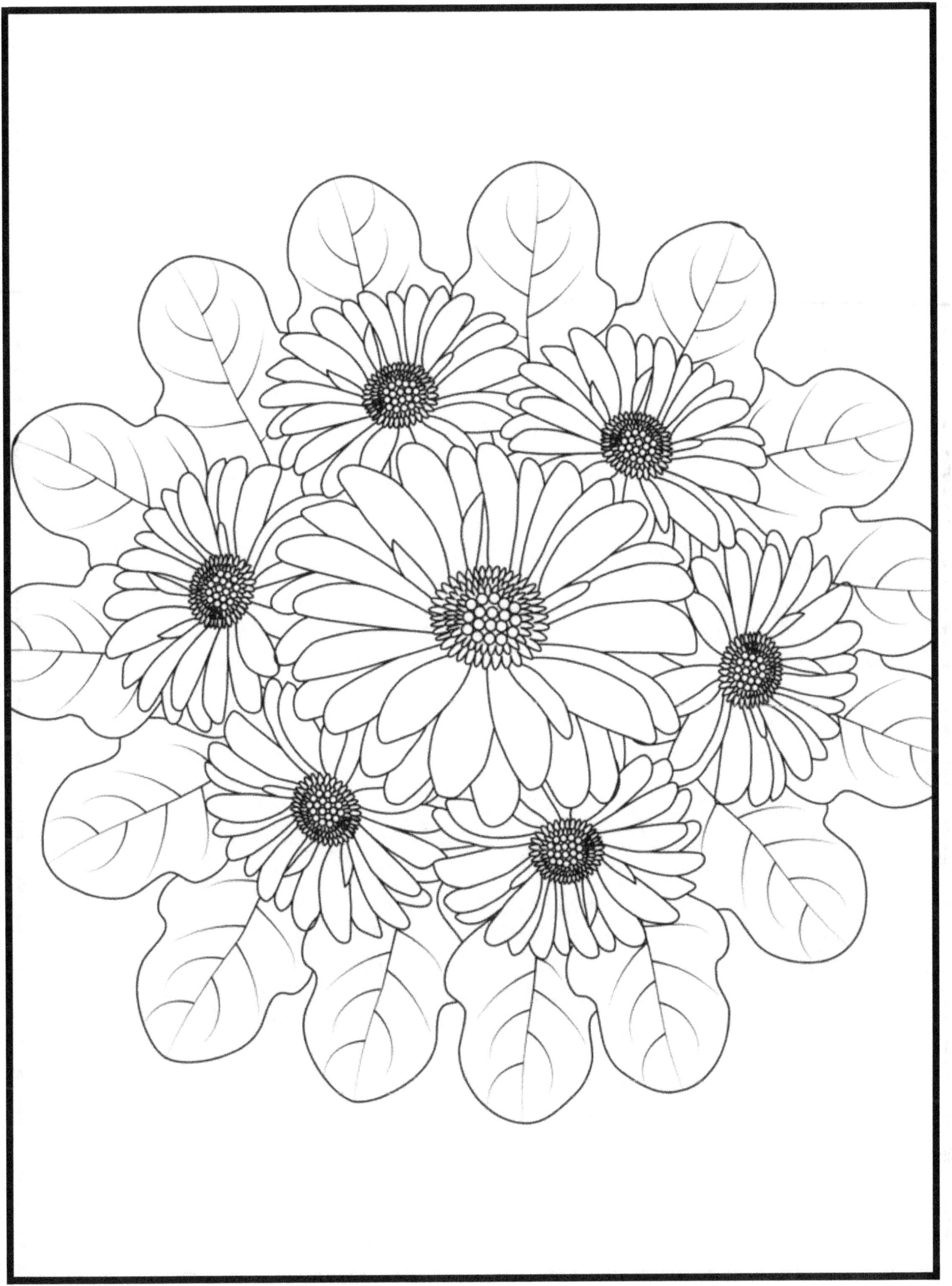

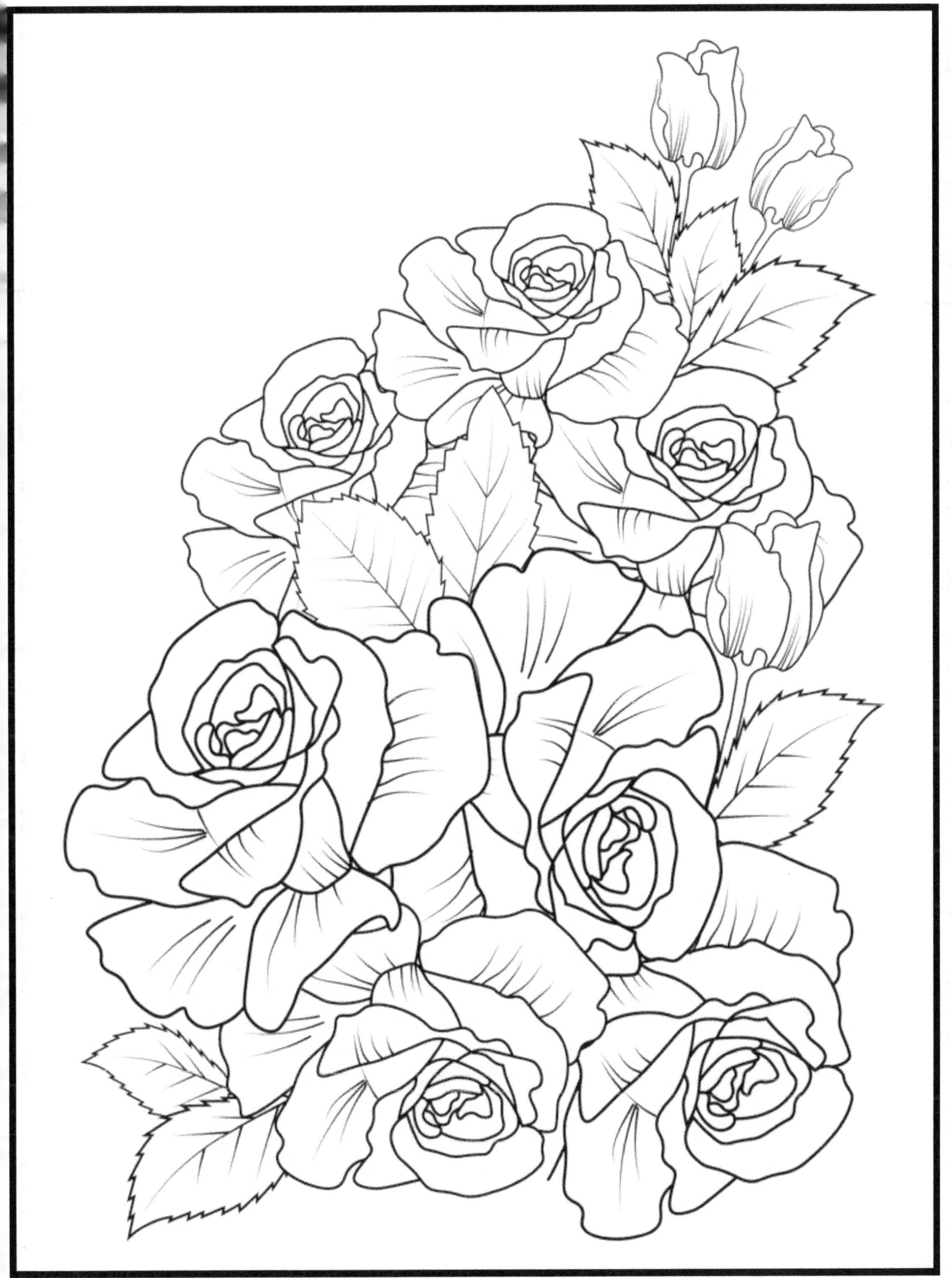

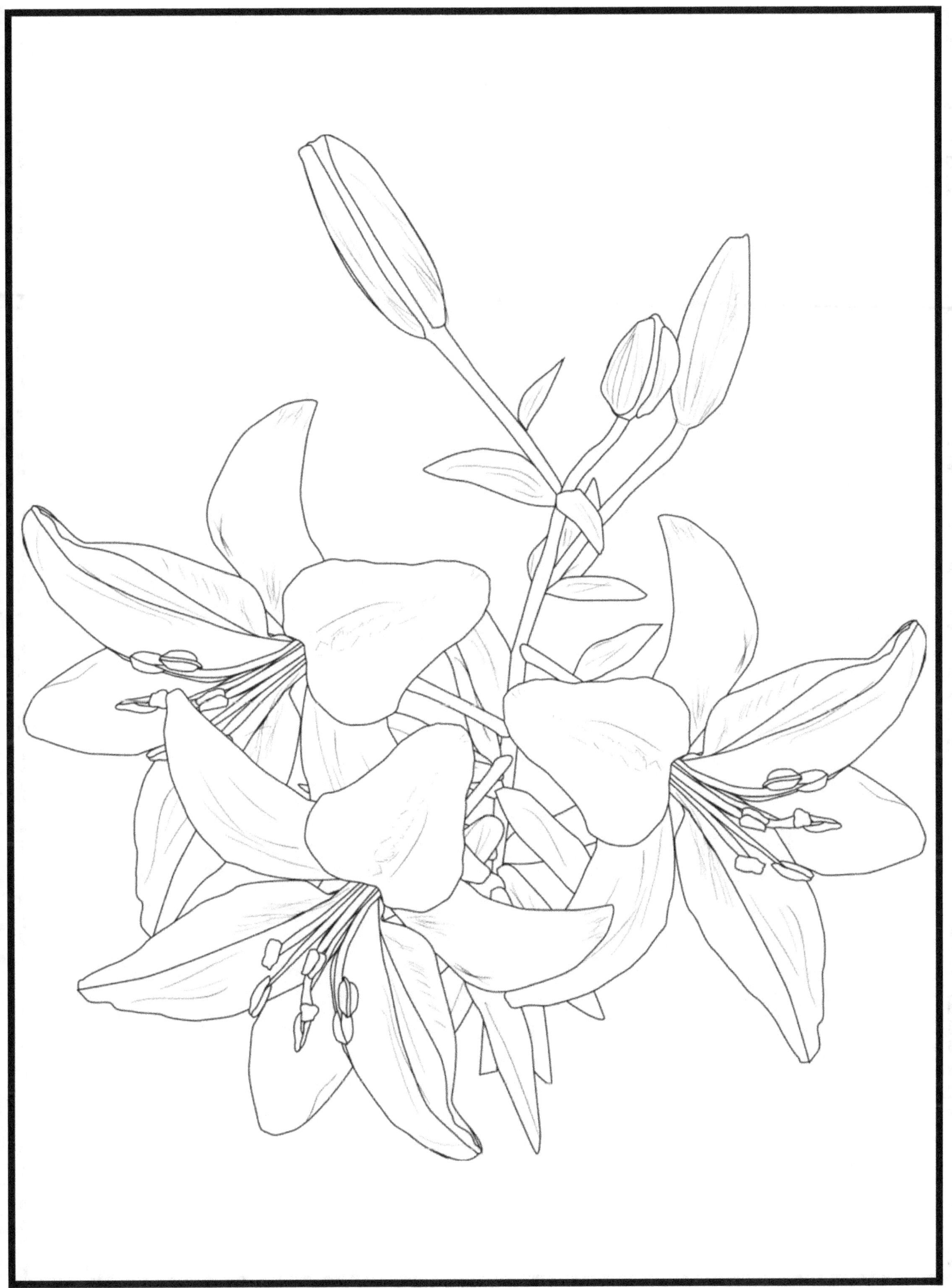

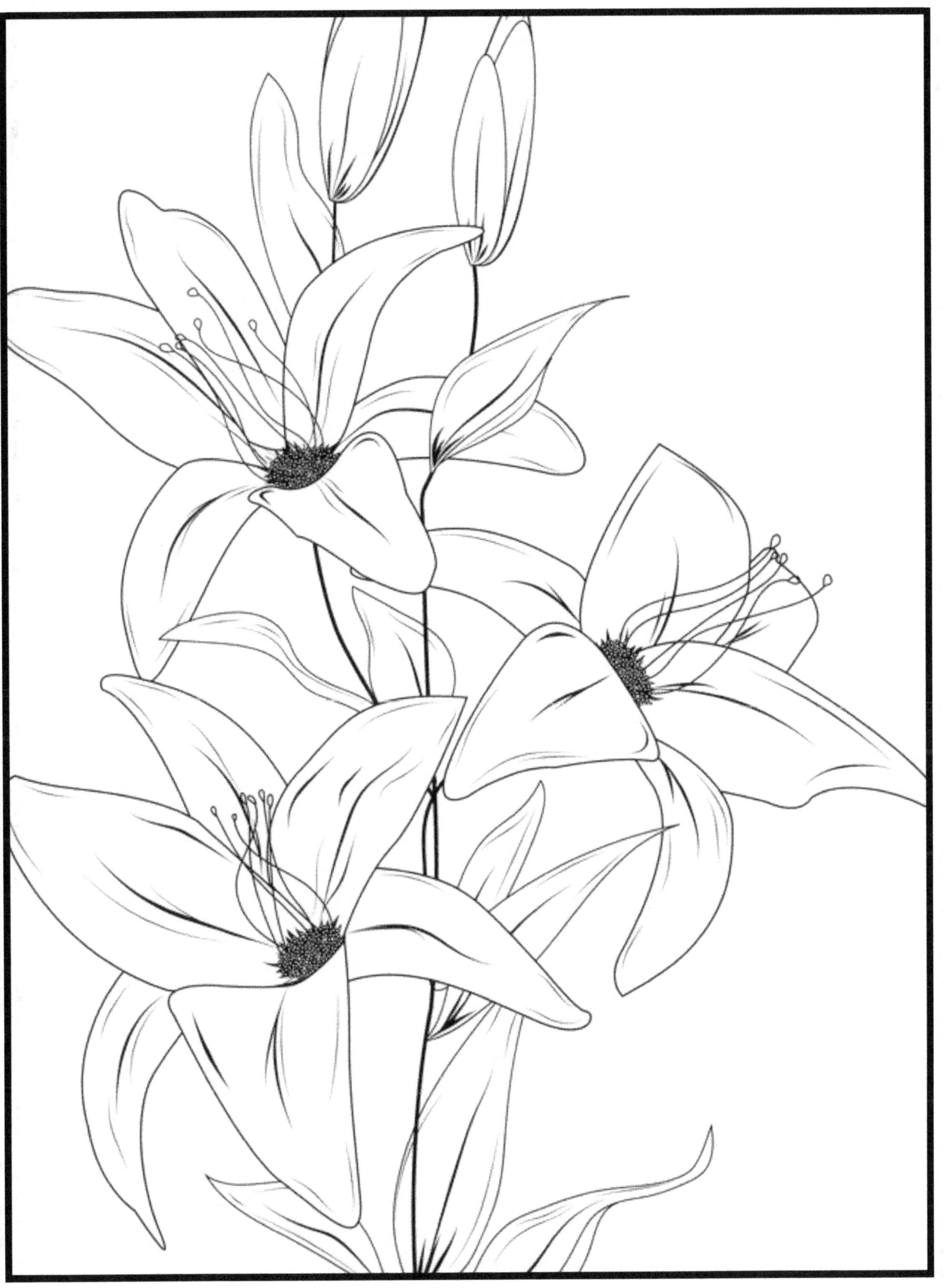

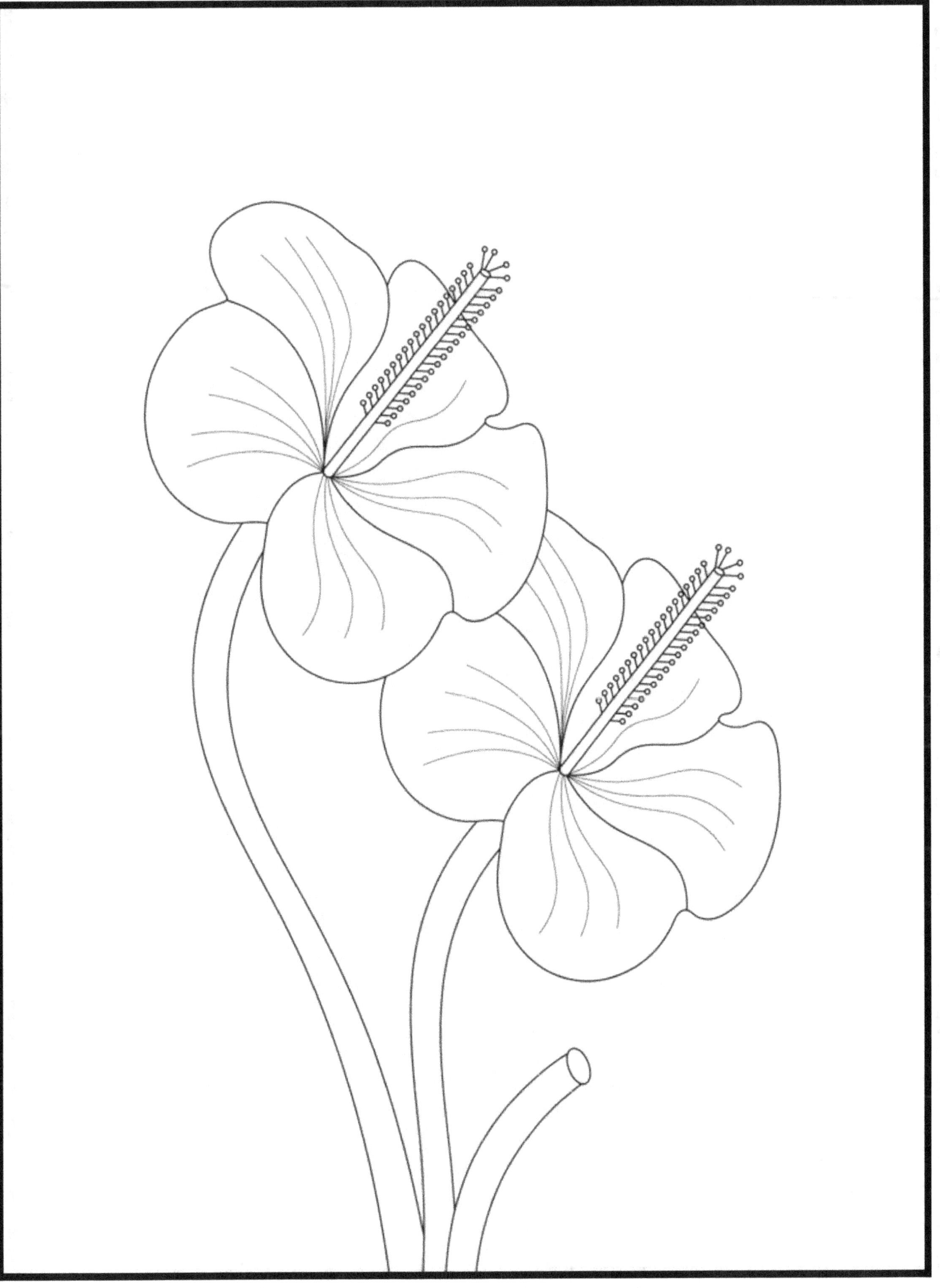

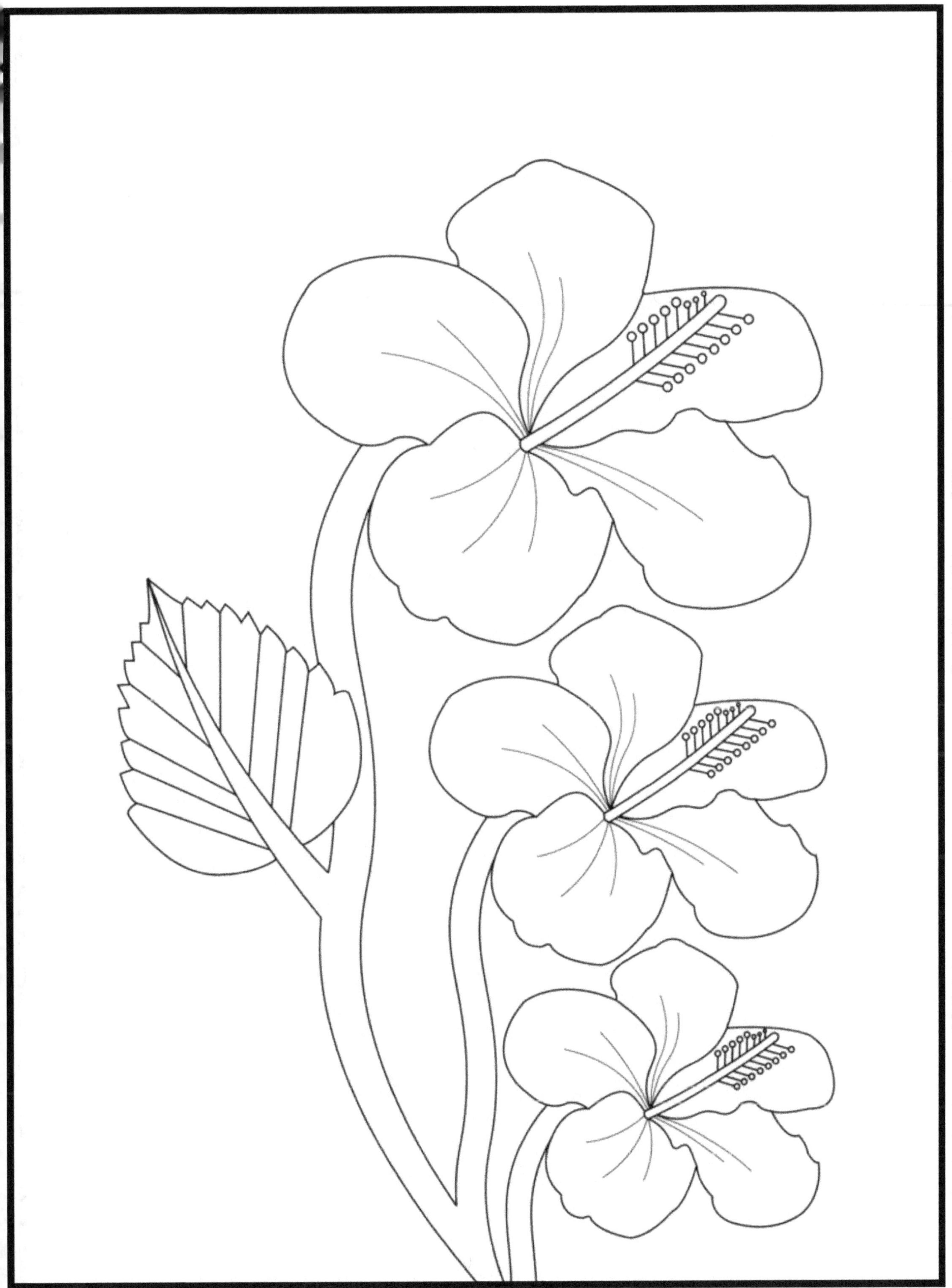

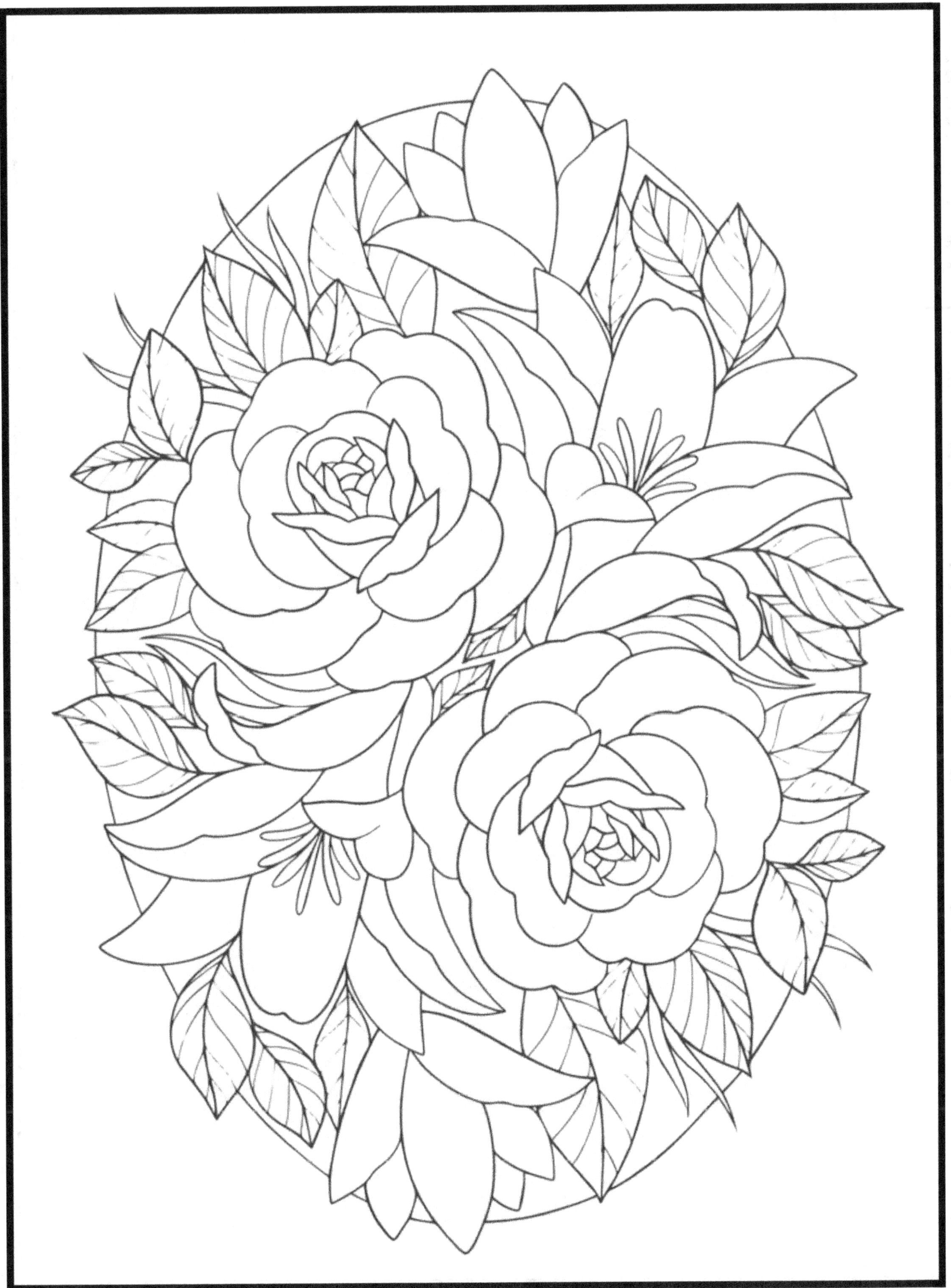

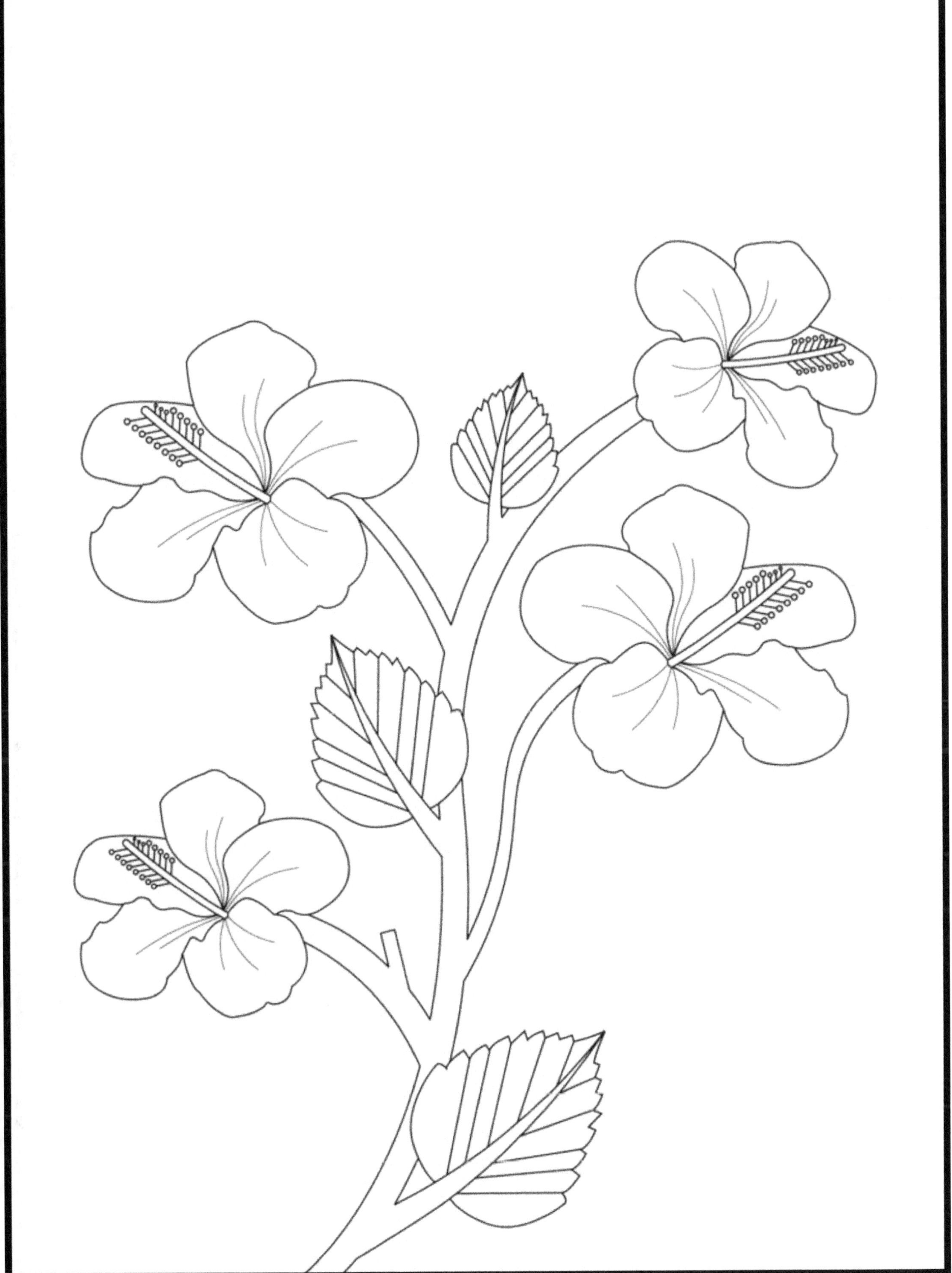

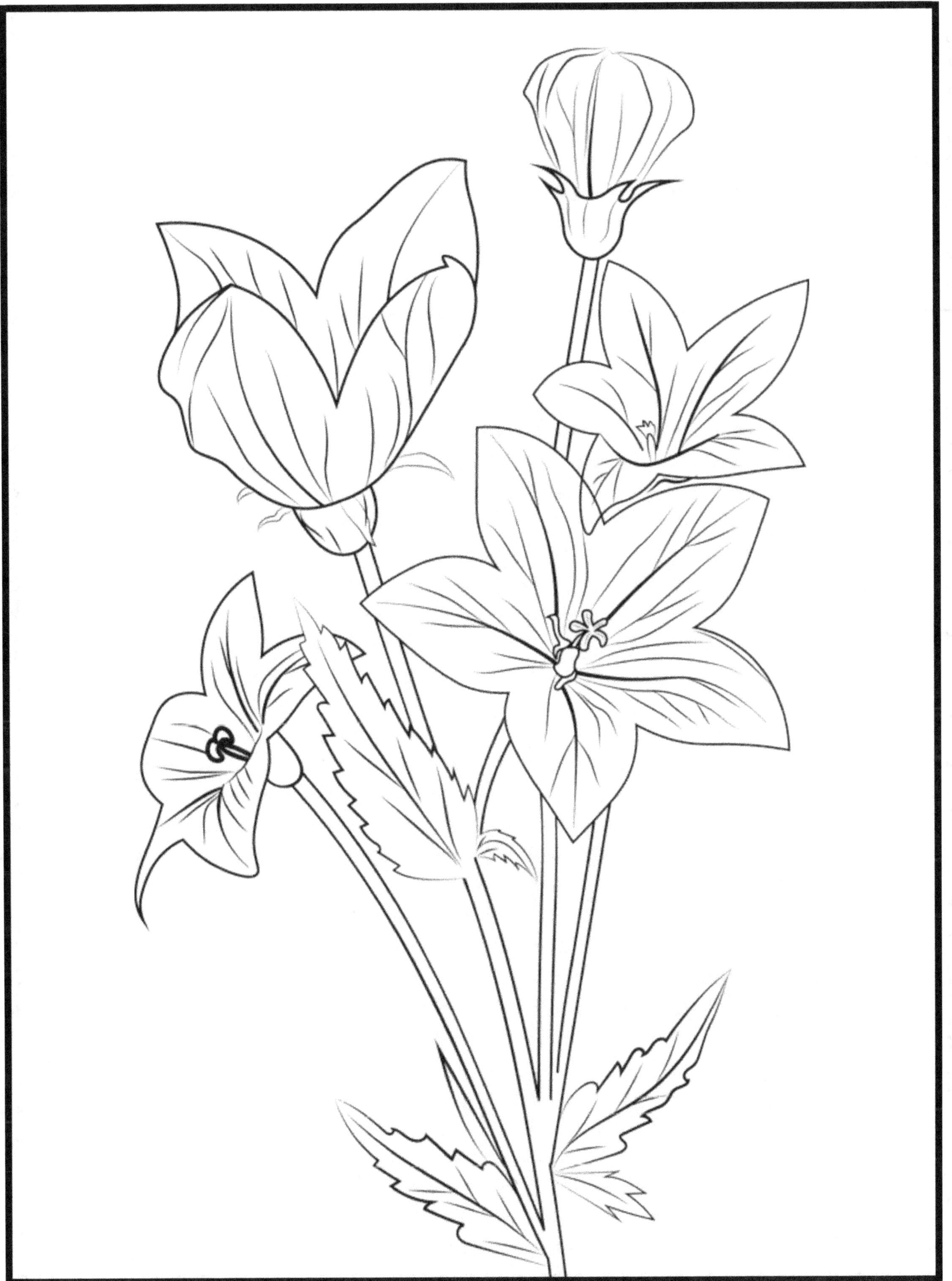

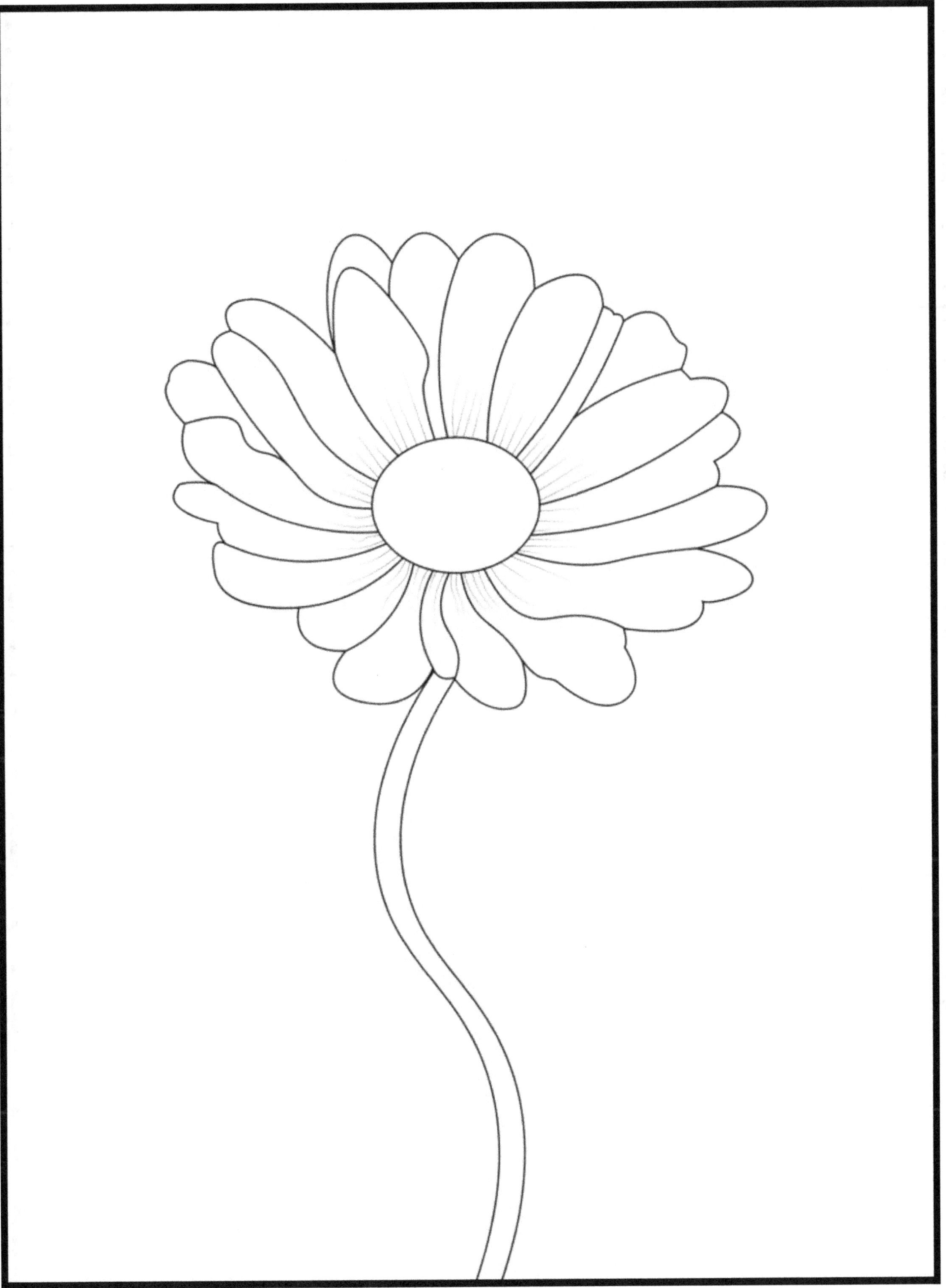

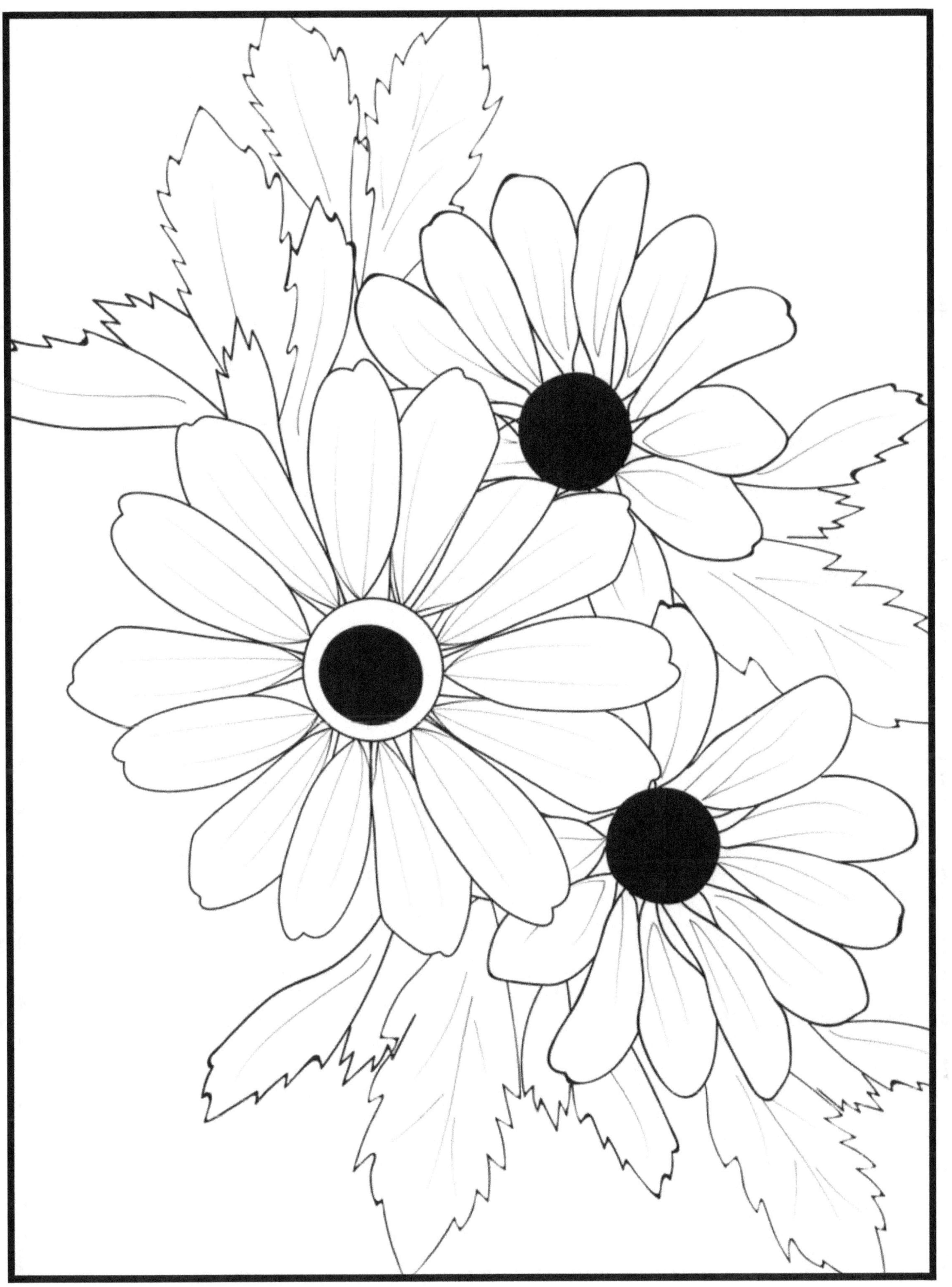

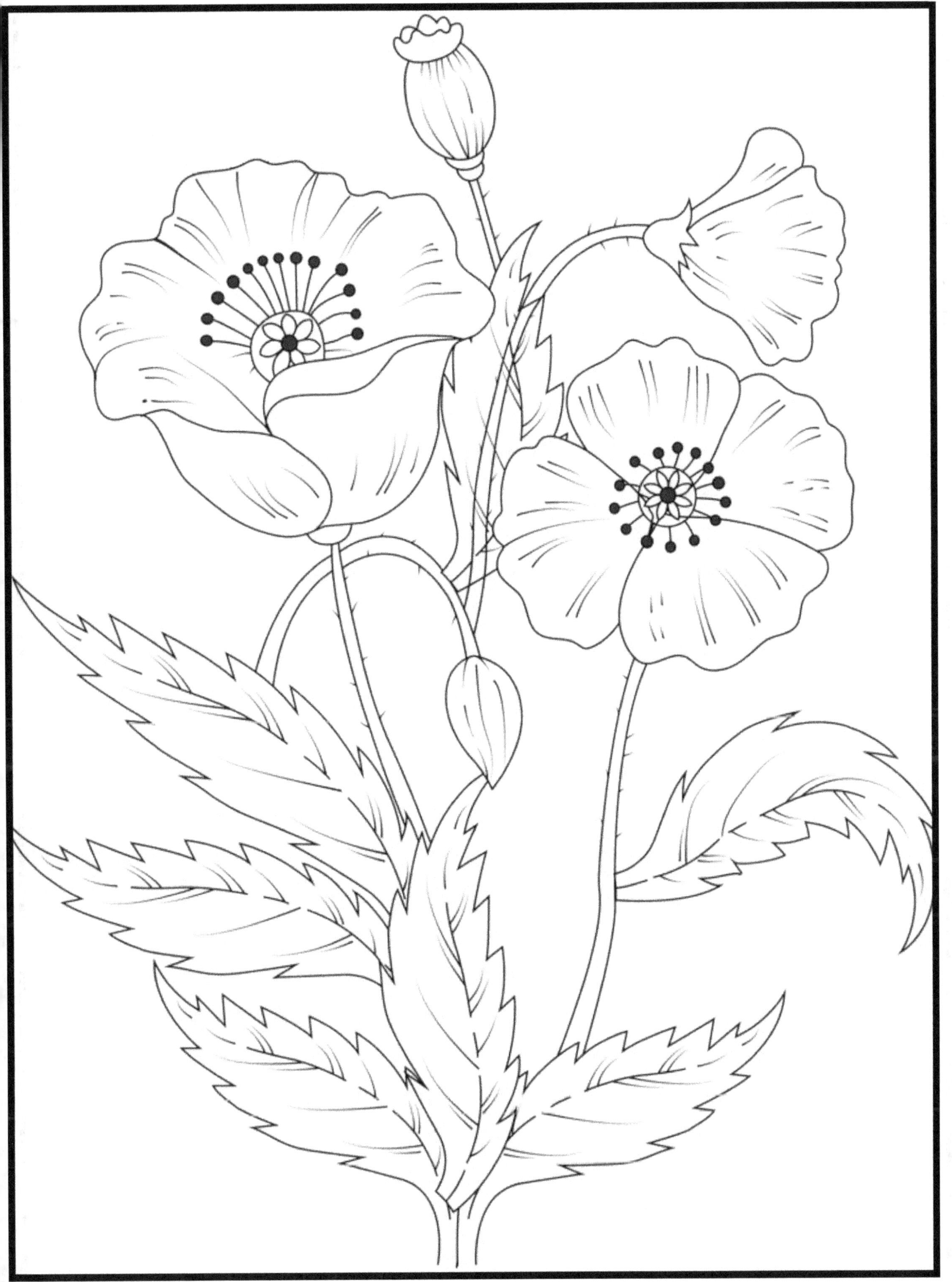

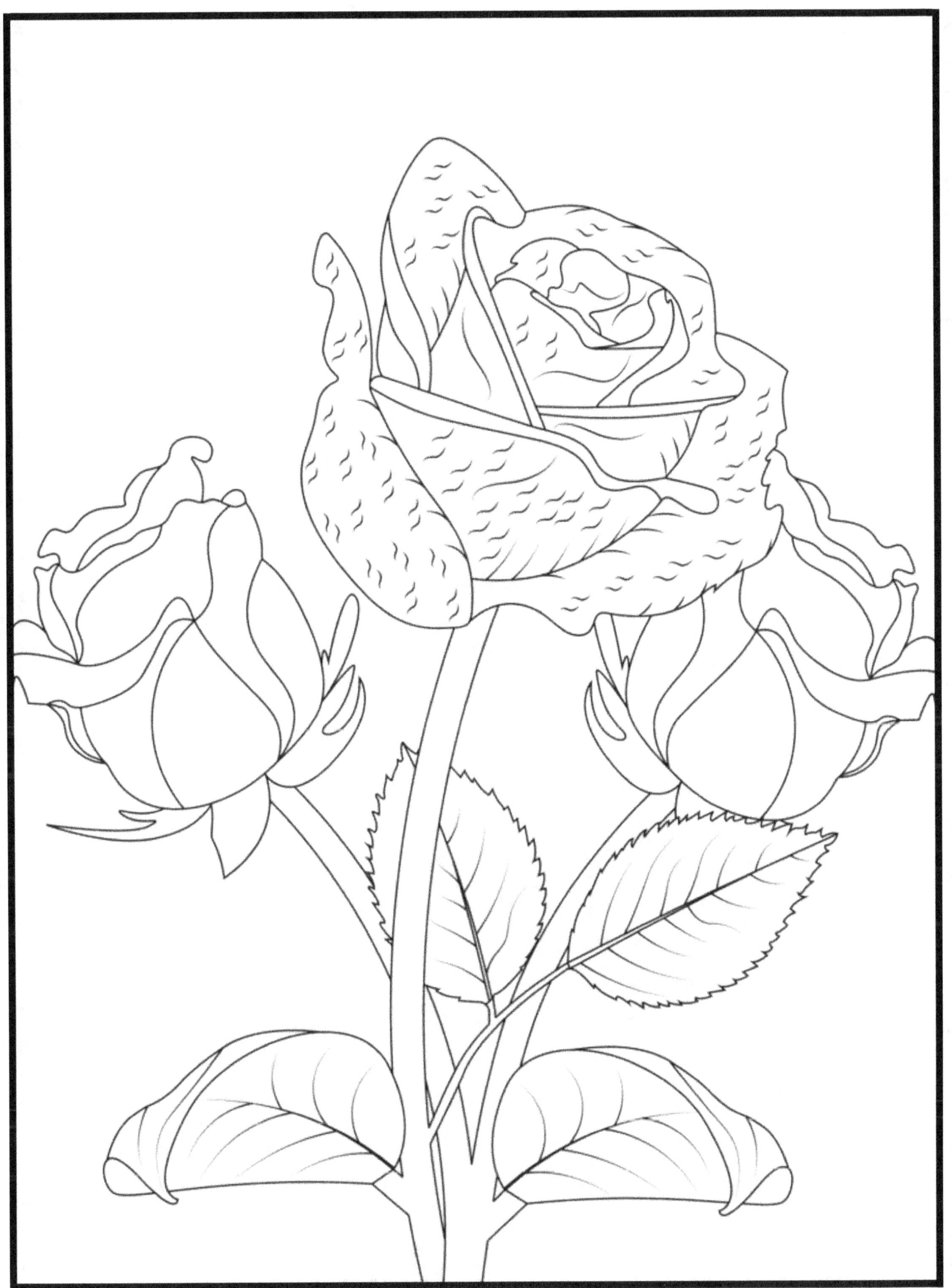

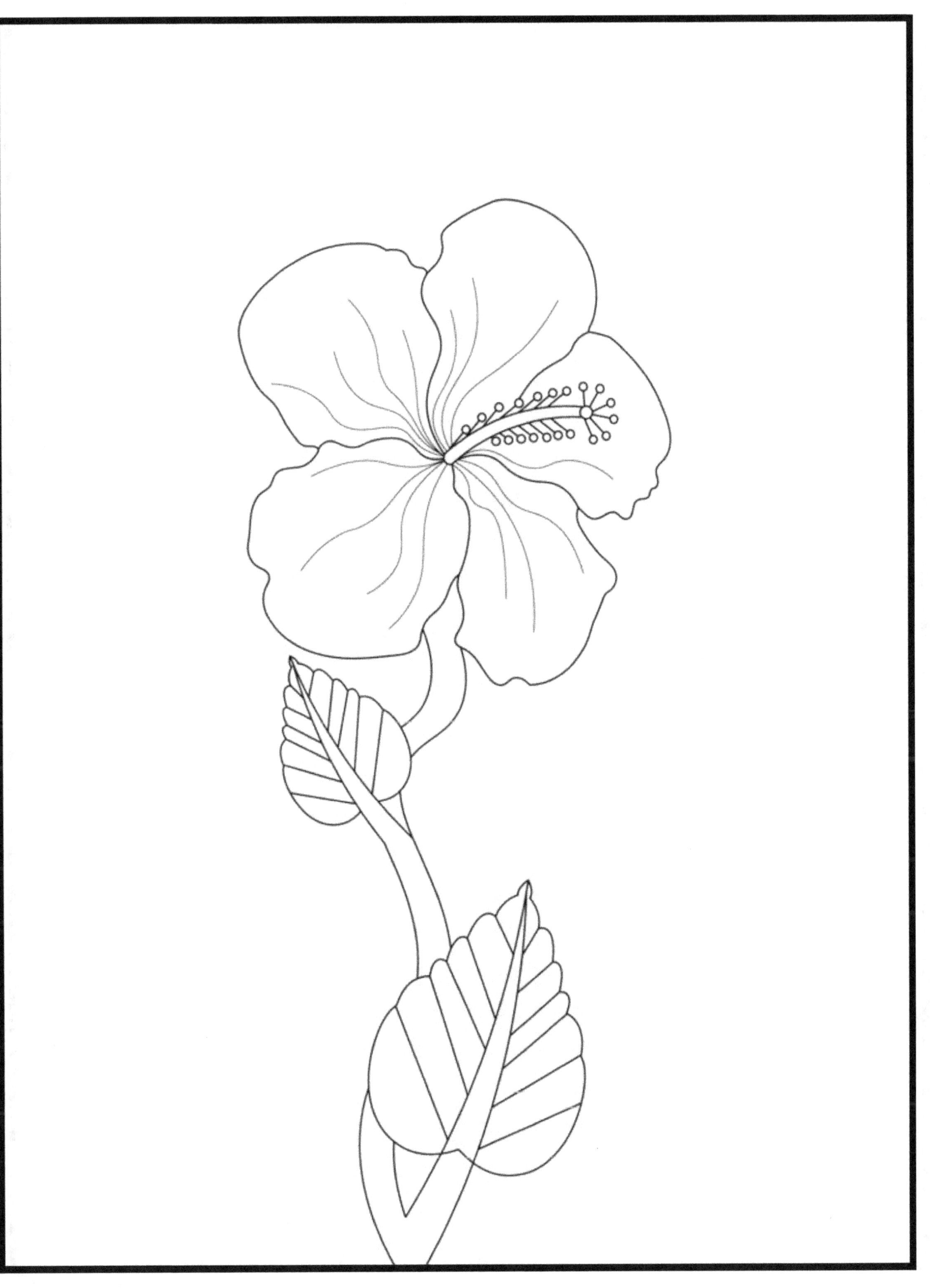

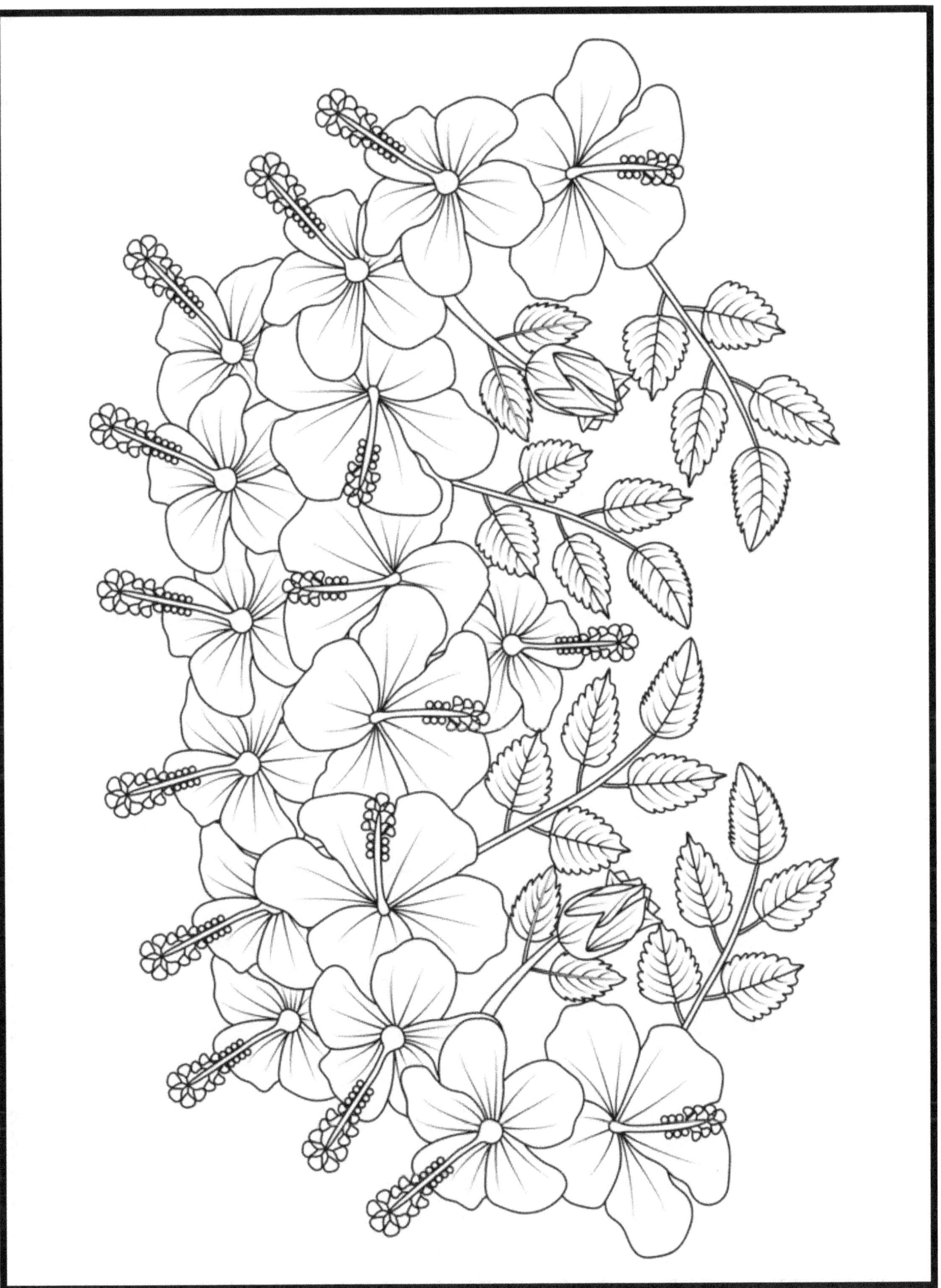

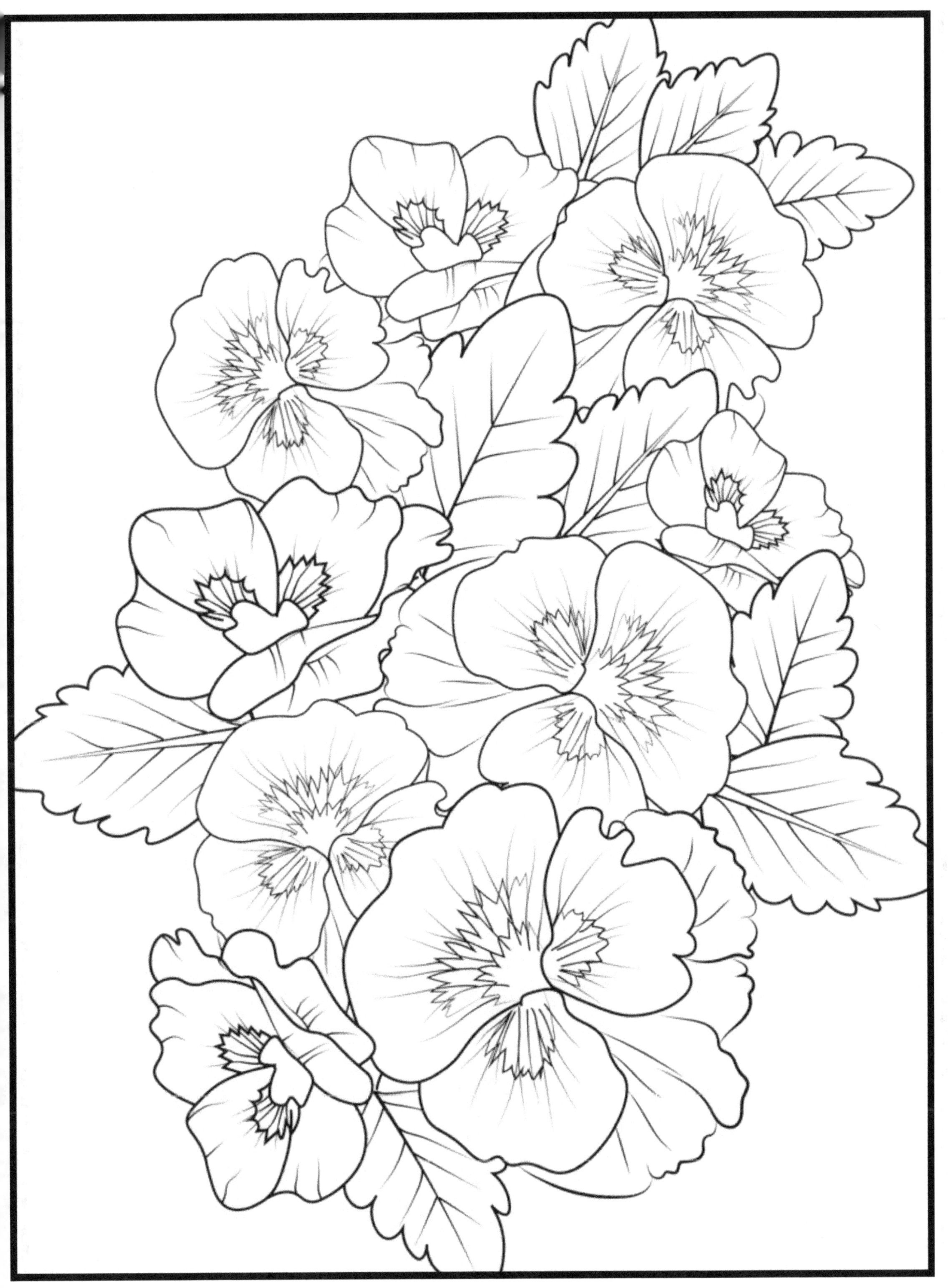

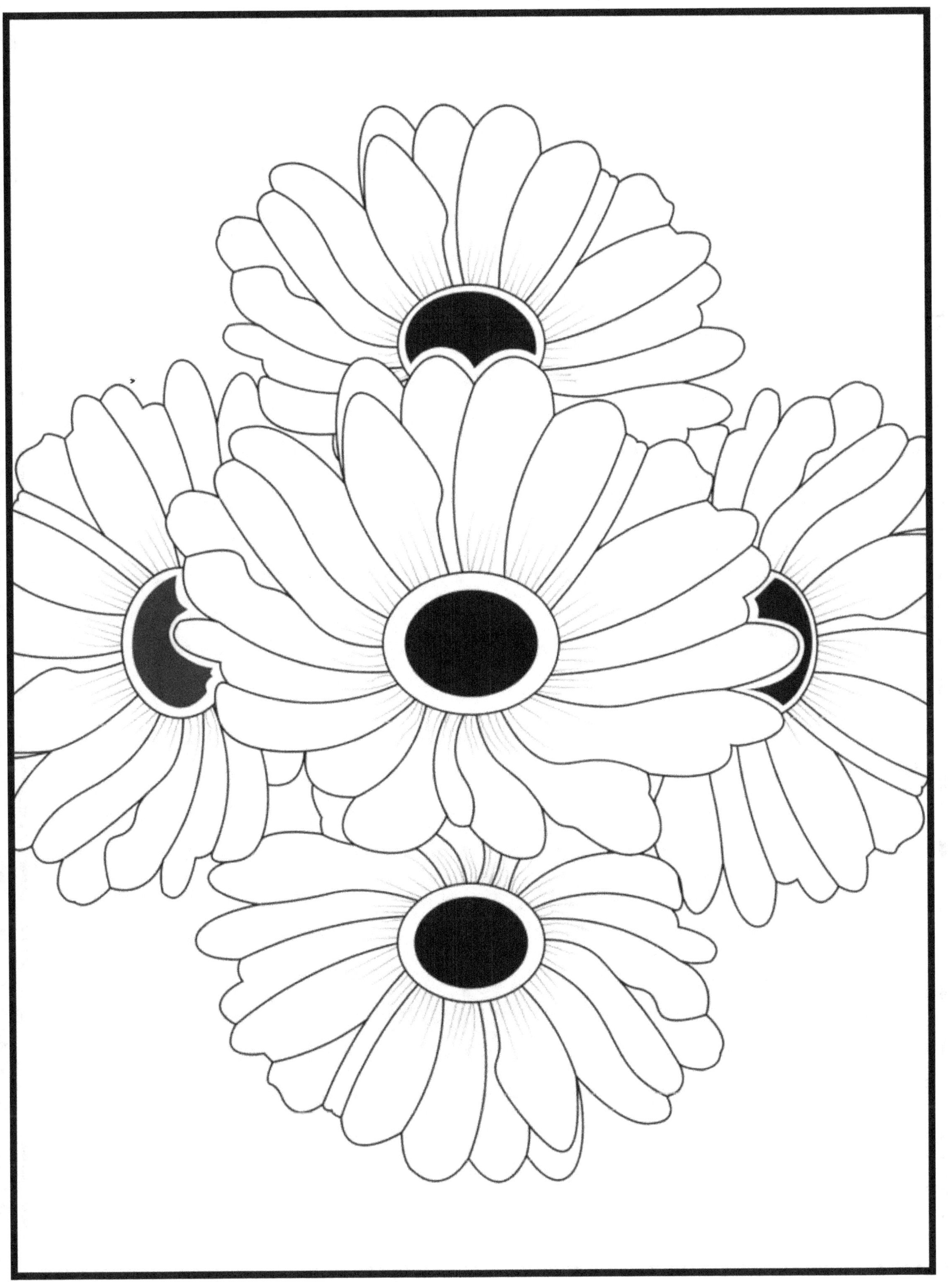